Science 4
Student Guide

Part 2

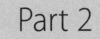

About K12 Inc.

K12 Inc., a technology-based education company, is the nation's leading provider of proprietary curriculum and online education programs to students in grades K–12. K¹² provides its curriculum and academic services to online schools, traditional classrooms, blended school programs, and directly to families. K12 Inc. also operates the K¹² International Academy, an accredited, diploma-granting online private school serving students worldwide. K¹²'s mission is to provide any child the curriculum and tools to maximize success in life, regardless of geographic, financial, or demographic circumstances. K12 Inc. is accredited by CITA. More information can be found at www.K12.com.

978-1-60153-337-1

Printed by Courier, Kendallville, IN, USA, April 2013, Lot 042013

Table of Contents

Unit 9: Weathering, Erosion, and Deposition

Unit 10: Fossils and Geologic Time

Student Guide
Lesson 1: Classifying Animals

What do a spotted ladybug, an octopus, and a sea urchin all have in common? These organisms are *invertebrates*--organisms that don't have a backbone. Meet other organisms and discover the world of invertebrates as you read *Come Learn With Me: Animals Without Backbones: Invertebrates*.

How are invertebrates different from vertebrates? How are they grouped in the Kingdom Animalia? Venture into the world of invertebrates and discover for yourself!

Lesson Objectives

- Explain that living things are sorted into different groups based on certain common characteristics.
- State that *vertebrates* are organisms that have a backbone.
- State that *invertebrates* are organisms that do not have a backbone.
- Recognize that invertebrates are not a single taxonomic group but are represented in many groups.

PREPARE

Approximate lesson time is 60 minutes.

Advance Preparation

- You will need the book *Animals Without Backbones: Invertebrates,* by Bridget Anderson, for all the lessons in this unit. If you have not yet received the book, skip to unit 7.

Materials

> For the Student
>> Come Learn with Me: Animals Without Backbones: Invertebrates by Bridget Anderson

Keywords and Pronunciation

anemone (uh-NEH-muh-nee)

Arthropoda (AHR-thruh-pah-duh) : The phylum of invertebrate animals, including insects and spiders, that have an exoskeleton, jointed legs, and a segmented body. More than 80 percent of all living species are arthropods.

Aurelia aurita (aw-REEL-ee-uh aw-RIY-tuh)

cell : The basic unit of all living things. There are many different types of cells in a living thing, each with a different job to do.

Chordata (kor-DAH-tuh)

classification : the process of dividing things into groups according to their characteristics

Cnidaria (niy-DAIR-ee-uh) : The phylum of aquatic, invertebrate animals that includes jellyfish and sea anemones.

exoskeleton (EK-soh-skeh-luh-tuhn) : The hard, outside body covering of an arthropod. The exoskeleton of the lobster protects the animal from predators in the ocean.

insect : An arthropod with three pairs of jointed legs and three body segments. Ants, grasshoppers, and mosquitoes are all insects.

invertebrate : An animal without a backbone. Sea stars, segmented worms, and spiders are classified as invertebrates because they don't have a backbone.

Kingdom Animalia : One of the six main groups into which all living things are divided. Most organisms in the animal kingdom are capable of movement, contain a nervous system, and take in food to produce energy.

phyla (FIY-luh) : Large groups of organisms that share similar characteristics. Phyla are the primary divisions within any kingdom. The singular of phyla is phylum.

phylogenetic (fiy-loh-juh-NEH-tihk)

species (SPEE-sheez) : A group of organisms that have many characteristics in common. The smallest and most specific groups that animals can be divided into are called species.

vertebrate (VUR-tuh-bruht) : An animal with a backbone. Mammals, fish, and birds are classified as vertebrates because they have a backbone.

LEARN
Activity 1: Let's Read! *(Online)*
What would your life be like if you didn't have a backbone? Ninety-five percent of animals on Earth don't have one. Learn about these animals and the world they inhabit.

Activity 2: Invertebrate Hunt *(Online)*
An *invertebrate* is an organism without a backbone. What invertebrates live near you?

Safety
As always, you may wish to preview any websites before your student views them.

ASSESS
Lesson Assessment: Classifying Animals (*Offline*)
You will complete an online assessment covering the main objectives of this lesson. Your assessment will be scored by the computer.

Student Guide
Lesson 2: The World of Sponges

Did you know that the original cleaning sponges were actually the skeletons of sponge animals? Enjoy the book and learn more about these fascinating creatures.

Lesson Objectives

- Identify characteristics of sponges (they have the ability to regenerate damaged parts, they reproduce through budding, and they live only in water).
- Identify the parts of a sponge (ostium, canal, osculum, and flagellum).

PREPARE

Approximate lesson time is 60 minutes.

Materials

For the Student

Come Learn with Me: Animals Without Backbones: Invertebrates by Bridget Anderson

🖳 Sponges

Keywords and Pronunciation

budding : A method of reproduction in which pieces of a sponge break off and develop into new sponges. A sponge produces many spores and regenerates through budding.

flagella (fluh-JEH-luh) : Tail-like structures on a cell that move back and forth. The flagella pushed the water through the canal of the sponge.

larva : The early life stage of certain animals that are not fully developed. When the egg of an insect hatches, the larva emerges.

osculum (AHS-kyuh-luhm) : A large pore through which filtered water leaves the body of a sponge. Sponges pump water through the canal of the sponge and out through the osculum.

ostium : The tiny pores, or holes, on the outer layer of a sponge. The ostium on the outer layer of the sponge allows water to enter into the canal of the sponge.

Porifera (paw-RIF-uhr-uh) : The phylum of the simple, invertebrate animals called sponges. The barrel sponge, vase sponge, and red beard sponge are part of the phylum Porifera.

regenerate : To grow back or repair parts that have been damaged. Sponges have the ability to regenerate body parts that may have been damaged by a predator.

spicules (SPIH-kyools) : Tiny fibers or minerals that make up the skeleton of a sponge. Within the jelly-like layer of a sponge cell is a network of needle-like spicules that form the skeleton of the sponge.

LEARN
Activity 1: Let's Read! *(Online)*
Sponges have a lot of practical uses, but the really interesting sponges aren't found in the kitchen or bathroom. Sponges live in oceans and other bodies of water, and they are living things that can move.

Activity 2: The Parts of a Sponge *(Online)*
Sponges have special features that make them unlike any other phylum. Investigate the parts of a sponge to discover how sponges are different from other organisms.

The sponge is an animal that has many different parts--each with a different job.
Use the book to label the parts of the sponge on the Sponge sheet. The labels for the parts of the sponge are in the Word Bank at the top of the sheet.
Then, below the picture, use the words to describe how water enters and exits the sponge's body cavity. You may use the book as a guide if you wish.

ASSESS
Lesson Assessment: The World of Sponges (*Online*)
You will complete an online assessment covering the main objectives of this lesson. Your assessment will be scored by the computer.

Name _____   Date _____

Sponges

1. Using the words in the Word Bank, label the parts of the sponge.

Word Bank				
canal	flagella	osculum	ostia	spicule

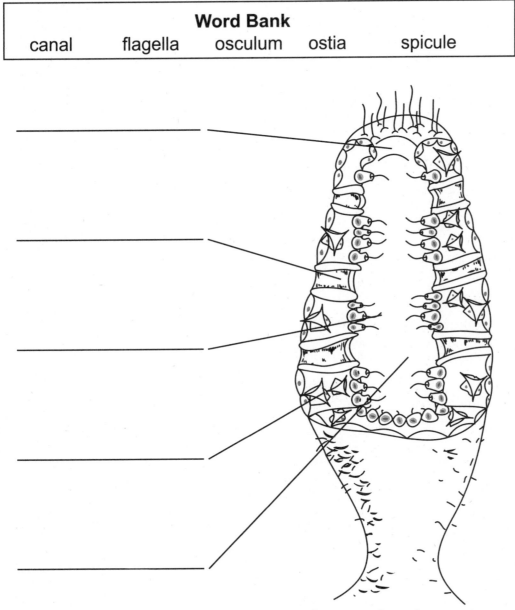

Cross section of a sponge

2. Use the words above to describe how water enters and exits the sponge's body cavity. _____
_____
_____

Student Guide
Lesson 3: Cnidarians

Have you ever been stung by a jellyfish? How are jellyfish able to do that? Learn more about the phylum Cnidaria, which includes interesting creatures such as jellyfish, sea anemones, and coral.

Lesson Objectives
- Identify a characteristic of cnidarians (they have tentacles with stinging cells).
- Identify medusa and polyp as the two common body types of cnidarians.
- Identify the three functions of tentacles (to sting predators, sense the environment, and bring food into the animal's mouth).
- State that most cnidarians help build up coral reefs.

PREPARE

Approximate lesson time is 60 minutes.

Materials
For the Student

Come Learn with Me: Animals Without Backbones: Invertebrates by Bridget Anderson

📖 Cnidaria Chart

Keywords and Pronunciation
anemone (uh-NEH-muh-nee)
Cnidaria (niy-DAIR-ee-uh) : The phylum of aquatic, invertebrate animals that includes jellyfish and sea anemones.
medusa : A body form of cnidarians. Medusae float freely through the water.
mutualism (MYOO-chuh-wuh-lih-zuhm) : A relationship between two animals in which both animals benefit. Clownfish and sea anemones live together to help each other survive. This relationship is known as mutualism.
polyp (PAH-luhp) : A body form of cnidarians. A polyp attaches to rocks, shells, or the sea floor by its feet-like structures.

LEARN
Activity 1: Let's Read! *(Online)*
If you've spent a lot of time near oceans, you've probably seen cnidarians. You might also see them in rivers or lakes. Curious swimmers who come too close to these beautiful animals learn a lesson--cnidarians can defend themselves!

Activity 2: Characteristics of Cnidarians *(Online)*

Jellyfish, sea anemones, hydra, and corals are all cnidarians, but they have their differences. Compare these animals' appearance, movements, homes, and unique characteristics.

ASSESS

Lesson Assessment: Cnidarians (*Online*)

You will complete an online assessment covering the main objectives of this lesson. Your assessment will be scored by the computer.

LEARN

Activity 3: Search for Cnidarians *(Online)*

Search the waters of the deep to explore the diverse world of cnidarians.

Name _____   Date _____

Cnidarian Chart

Complete the missing parts of the chart.

1. SEA ANEMONE

How It Looks:

_____

_____

How It Moves:
it waves from the ocean floor

Where It Lives:

_____

Something That Makes It Unique:

_____

_____

2. JELLYFISH

How It Looks:
**some look like umbrellas, and
some look like lion manes**

How It Moves:

_____

Where It Lives:

_____

Something That Makes It Unique:

_____

_____

3. HYDRA

How It Looks:

_____

_____

How It Moves:

_____

Where It Lives:
in fresh water

Something That Makes It Unique:

_____

_____

4. STONY CORAL

How It Looks:

_____

_____

How It Moves:

_____

Where It Lives:

_____

Something That Makes It Unique:
**new corals grow on top of old
ones**

Student Guide
Lesson 4: The Diverse World of Worms

What comes to your mind when you think of worms? Soil? Slimy? There are more types of worms than the common earthworm most people think of. Look deep into the diverse world of worms. You'll be surprised at how many different kinds of worms there are in the soil, in the oceans, and in freshwater!

Lesson Objectives

- Identify characteristics of roundworms (they bend from side to side to move, have nostrils but no eyes).
- Compare segmented worms to roundworms and flatworms.
- Identify a characteristic of segmented worms (their body is made up of many ring-like segments).
- Identify characteristics of flatworms (they have eyespots and the ability to regenerate when damaged).
- State that the term *worm* is used for animals in three different phyla.

PREPARE

Approximate lesson time is 60 minutes.

Materials

> For the Student
>
>> Come Learn with Me: Animals Without Backbones: Invertebrates by Bridget Anderson
>
> 💻 Characteristics of Worms Chart

Keywords and Pronunciation

Annelida (A-nluh-duh) : The phylum of invertebrate animals that includes earthworms and all other segmented worms. Earthworms, bristle worms, and leeches are part of the phylum Annelida.

cuticle : The protective layer of skin on worms. The muscles of a roundworm are covered with a skin that produces a tough layer called the cuticle.

ganglion (GANG-glee-uh) : A simple, brain-like organ in some animals. In a flatworm, the eyespots are connected to the ganglia, which process information from the eyespots.

Nematoda (NEH-muh-toh-duh) : The phylum of invertebrate animals that includes roundworms. Nematoda live wherever ther is water.

planarian (pluh-NAIR-ee-uhn) : A nonparasitic flatworm that lives in freshwater. A planarian, a type of flatworm, can regenerate its body even when it has been cut into many pieces.

Platyhelminthes : The phylum of invertebrate animals that includes more than 20,000 species of flatworms. Platyhelminthes means flat worm in Greek.

LEARN
Activity 1: Let's Read! *(Online)*

Unlike cnidarians, worms have heads and tails. Worms live in many settings, from gardens to inside animals and people. Learn about three more phyla: Platyhelminthes, Nematoda, and Annelida.

Activity 2: Characteristics of Worms *(Offline)*

Are all worms the same? Do worms that live in the soil have anything in common with worms that live in coral reefs? Use a chart to find out how the three worm phyla are related.

Safety

As always, you may wish to view recommended websites before your student views them.

ASSESS

Lesson Assessment: The Diverse World of Worms (*Online*)

You will complete an online assessment covering the main objectives of this lesson. Your assessment will be scored by the computer.

LEARN
Activity 3. Optional: A Visit to Worm World *(Online)*

Did you know earthworms have five hearts? Why is a worm considered a recycler? Dig deep into this site for more information about the world of worms.

Name _____   Date _____

Characteristics of Worms Chart

The worms listed below belong to different phyla, so they have similarities as well as differences. Use pages 24-29 of the text to find the specific characteristics of each type of worm. Look at the characteristics listed below, then decide which characteristics apply to each worm. Write "yes" in the chart if the worm has the characteristic; write "no" if it does not. Three have been completed for you.

Characteristics	Worms		
	Roundworms	Flatworms	Segmented Worms
Eyespots connected to ganglia			
Able to regenerate if their body is damaged			Some do
Long, slender, round bodies			
Flat bodies			
Segmented bodies			
Nostrils			
Head and tail			
Bend from side to side in order to move		Yes	No

Use the information in the chart to compare segmented worms to roundworms and flatworms.

_____

_____

_____

_____

_____

Student Guide
Lesson 5: Mighty Mollusks

We are all familiar with snails and slugs--they are mollusks. But an octopus is a mollusk too, and it seems quite different from a slug. Add to these animals the squid that moves through water, leaving an inky blackness, and you have a very diverse group of animals. What characteristics do these soft-bodied and often hard-shelled animals have in common?

Lesson Objectives

- Identify characteristics of mollusks (they have a soft body, a thick skin called a mantle, and a foot for movement).
- Identify three ways mollusks can move (using a foot extended from their body, filling their shell with air to float away, pulling with their arms, or taking water in and pushing it out of the siphon).
- Identify characteristics of snails and slugs (they have stalked eyes, antennae, radula, and a foot on the underside of the belly for movement).
- Identify characteristics of clams, mussels, and oysters (they have two shells joined by a hinge, a siphon, and a foot for movement).
- Identify characteristics of octopuses and squids (they have a large brain, highly developed eyes, and long arm-like appendages).

PREPARE

Approximate lesson time is 60 minutes.

Materials

> For the Student

> > Come Learn with Me: Animals Without Backbones: Invertebrates by Bridget Anderson

> > 🖳 Mollusca Crossword Puzzle

Keywords and Pronunciation

bivalve : A mollusk that has two shells connected by a hinge. Clams have two shells connected by a hinge, so they are bivalves.

cephalopod (SEH-fuh-luh-pahd) : A mollusk that can swim and has appendages on its head. An octopus can swim and has tentacles, so it is a cephalopod.

gastropod (GAS-truh-pahd) : A mollusk that has a foot attached to its underbelly. Most gastropods, including snails, have a single spiral shell. Slugs have no shell at all.

mantle : A thick outer covering on a mollusk's body. In some mollusks, the mantle produces a shell.

Mollusca (muh-LUH-skuh) : The phylum of invertebrate animals that have a soft body, a muscular foot for movement, and a mantle. The oyster belongs to the phylum Mollusca.

radula (RA-juh-luh) : The tongue-like structure of many mollusks that is covered in a hard, tooth-like substance. When a mollusk feeds, its radula can remove algae from rocks.

siphon (SIY-fuhn) : In a bivalve, a tube used for breathing and feeding. A bivalve breathes and gets food by filtering the water that comes in through the siphon.

LEARN

Activity 1: Let's Read! *(Online)*

Oysters and clams actually have a soft body. A hard shell protects this vulnerable body. Learn what oysters and clams have in common with the snail, squid, octopus, and other sea animals.

Activity 2: Mollusca Puzzle *(Offline)*

Now that you know so many facts about mollusks, it's time to show off your knowledge. The Mollusca Crossword Puzzle will help you to do this. Use your book to help you find the answers.

ASSESS

Lesson Assessment: Mighty Mollusks (*Online*)

You will complete an online assessment covering the main objectives of this lesson. Your assessment will be scored by the computer.

Name _____   Date _____

Mollusca Crossword Puzzle

Use the clues on the next page to complete the puzzle.

Mollusca Crossword Puzzle

ACROSS

1. This word means "two shells."

2. It has two shells and produces pearls. It also has a siphon.

5. This gastropod has to move its foot and head out of its shell to move.

6. Its shell is lighter than those of other mollusks.

7. Snails and slugs are part of this mollusk group.

9. This bivalve can breathe under mud.

13. This cephalopod hides from enemies by squeezing into tiny places. It has a highly developed brain.

14. Cephalopods such as squid _____ by taking water into their bodies and pushing it out throught their siphons

15. A gastropod's eyes are mounted at the end of these.

16. This word means "head foot."

DOWN

3. This is the "tongue" of a gastropod.

4. This connects the halves of a bivalve.

8. This shy cephalopod moves quickly and has very good eyesight.

10. This type of slug can grow more than 15cm long.

11. This phylum is Latin for "soft one." Members of this phylum have soft bodies and a mantle.

12. Created by a snail's foot, this helps the snail glide over flat surfaces.

Student Guide
Lesson 6: Arthropods

A spider crawls up a waterspout as a bee moves gracefully around a flower. In the earth a millipede moves through the loose litter of fallen leaves. In a nearby creek, a crayfish grasps at a meal with its claws. What do all these animals have in common? They are *arthropods,* animals with a segmented body and jointed legs.

Lesson Objectives

- Identify common characteristics of arthropods (they have jointed legs, a segmented body, and an exoskeleton).
- Identify characteristics of insects (they have three pairs of legs, three body segments--head, thorax, and abdomen--and one or two pairs of wings).
- Identify characteristics of crustaceans (they have five pairs of jointed legs, two pairs of antenna, and an exoskeleton).

PREPARE

Approximate lesson time is 60 minutes.

Materials

For the Student

Come Learn with Me: Animals Without Backbones: Invertebrates by Bridget Anderson

📖 Arthropods

Keywords and Pronunciation

abdomen (AB-duh-muhn) : The rear body section of an arthropod. The abdomen is the back end of an insect.

Arthropoda (AHR-thruh-pah-duh) : The phylum of invertebrates, including insects and spiders, that have an exoskeleton, jointed legs, and a segmented body. You can easily recognize arthropods by their hard, outer covering, known as the exoskeleton, and by their jointed legs.

cephalothorax (seh-fuh-luh-THOR-aks) : In arachnids, the front section of the body that includes the head. An arachnid's antennae are on the cephalothorax.

chiton (KIY-tuhn)

crustacean (crustacea) (kruhs-TAY-shuhn)

entomologist (en-tuh-MAH-luh-jist)

exoskeleton (EK-soh-skeh-luh-tuhn) : The hard, outside body covering of an arthropod. The exoskeleton of the crab protects the animal from predators.

head : The top or front part of the body. All insects have three body parts: the head, the thorax, and the abdomen.

metamorphosis (meh-tuh-MOR-fuh-suhs) : The series of changes in body shape that certain animals go through as they develop from eggs to adults. The metamorphosis of a frog is from egg to tadpole to adult frog.

spinneret : An organ in some invertebrates, including spiders, that produces silk. The spinneret releases a liquid silk that the spider uses to weave a web.

thorax (THOR-aks) : The middle body section of many arthropods. The thorax of an arthropod lies between the head and the abdomen.

LEARN
Activity 1: Let's Read! *(Online)*

Like mollusks, arthropods are protected by an outside skeleton. Unlike mollusks, however, arthropods have a segmented body. Discover the characteristics of the phylum Arthropoda.

Activity 2: What Makes Me an Arthropod? *(Offline)*

Crustaceans and insects are part of the phylum Arthropoda. Discover some similarities and differences between these two invertebrate groups.

The phylum *Arthropoda* is made up of a very diverse group of invertebrates. Can you name some? [1] Let' look at two smaller groups within the phylum Arthropoda. Smaller groups that make up a phylum are called *classes*. The first is the class of arthropods known as *insects*. Crustaceans, such as lobsters, make up another class. Look carefully back through the reading to compare crustaceans and insects. The Arthropods sheet will guide you to look for important information.

Answer:
[1] Answers will vary but may include these: tarantulas, butterflies, hermit crabs, and centipedes.

ASSESS

Lesson Assessment: Arthropods (*Online*)

You will complete an online assessment covering the main objectives of this lesson. Your assessment will be scored by the computer

---

LEARN
Activity 3. Optional: A Visit to the Museum *(Online)*

What does an entomologist study? Insects! Pick up the hand lens of an entomologist and get an up-close look at several insects, as well as other arthropods.

Safety

As always, you may wish to preview recommended websites before having your student view them.

Arthropods

1. Arthropods have three common characteristics. What are they?

   A. _____

   B. _____

   C. _____

2. Insects and crustaceans are two classes of arthropods. Fill in the chart to find out the characteristics that make each class unique.

	Insects	Crustaceans
How many pairs of jointed legs do they have?		
Their bodies are divided into what parts?		**head and thorax fused, abdomen**
Do some have wings?		
Do they have an exoskeleton?		
Do they have antennae?		**yes**

3. Label the body parts of the praying mantis and lobster.

Student Guide
Lesson 7: Echinoderms

What do sea stars, sea urchins, sand dollars, and sea cucumbers all have in common? They are all part of the phylum Echinodermata, meaning *spiny skin* in Greek. Take a closer look at these echinoderms and their common characteristics.

Lesson Objectives

- Identify characteristics of echinoderms (they are protected by hard plates, their body has radial symmetry, and they move by pumping water into their tube feet).
- Identify characteristics of sea stars (they live only in water, they have suction cups on their tube feet, their body has radial symmetry, and they are able to regenerate their body when it is damaged).

PREPARE

Approximate lesson time is 60 minutes.

Materials

For the Student

Come Learn with Me: Animals Without Backbones: Invertebrates by Bridget Anderson

🖥 Sea Stars

Keywords and Pronunciation

cephalothorax (seh-fuh-luh-THOR-aks) : In arachnids, the front section of the body that includes the head. An arachnid's antennae are on the cephalothorax.

crustacean (crustacea) (kruhs-TAY-shuhn)

echinoderm (ih-KIY-nuh-durm)

Echinodermata (ih-kiy-nuh-dur-MAH-tuh) : The phylum of aquatic invertebrates that are protected by a thick, spiny skin. Sea stars, sea urchins, and sand dollars are part of the phylum Echinodermata.

madreporite (MA-druh-por-iyt) : A small, circular plate that filters out debris. Water enters the madreporite on the top side of a sea star's central body and is pumped to the many feet on the bottom.

LEARN
Activity 1: Let's Read! *(Online)*

Sand dollars are not really money, though they look a lot like coins. They belong to the phylum Echinodermata, which means they have thick, spiny skin covered with plates. Like sea stars, their body is symmetrical around a central point. Learn about this phylum.

Activity 2: Sea Stars (*Online*)

Sea stars are quite unusual creatures. How do they move? How do they eat? Explore and find out!

ASSESS

Lesson Assessment: Echinoderms (*Online*)

You will complete an online assessment covering the main objectives of this lesson. Your assessment will be scored by the computer.

LEARN

Activity 3. Optional: A Closer Look into the Ocean (*Online*)

There are many different types of echinoderms that live deep in the world's oceans. Visit a gallery of photographs to take a look deep into the world of echinoderms.

Safety

As always, you may wish to preview recommended websites before your student views them.

Name _____ Date _____

Sea Stars

Review the Reading

Use the questions below to guide you as you re-read pages 44 – 45.

1. In what environment would you find a sea star? _____
   _____
   _____
   _____

2. What happened when fishermen found a sea star, chopped it up, and threw it back into the ocean? _____
   _____
   _____
   _____

3. The body of a sea star has radial symmetry. What does this mean? _____
   _____
   _____

4. Why is the sea star able to stay anchored on a rock, a coral, or the bottom of the ocean? _____
   _____
   _____

How a Sea Star Moves

On the website, view the movie clip titled "Sea Star Feeding." Then describe in your own words how a sea star moves. Refer to the reading as well as the text on the web page for help.

_____
_____
_____
_____
_____

Student Guide
Lesson 8: Unit Review and Assessment

What have you learned about invertebrates? Play a game and review all you know about this diverse world of organisms!

Lesson Objectives

- Identify different groups of invertebrates (sponges, cnidarians, worms, mollusks, arthropods, echinoderms) according to their common characteristics.

PREPARE

Approximate lesson time is 60 minutes.

Materials

For the Student

📖 Classification of Invertebrates Review Cards

Come Learn with Me: Animals Without Backbones: Invertebrates by Bridget Anderson

---

LEARN
Activity 1: Review the Reading *(Offline)*
Instructions

Take a moment to look back through the book. Look at the pictures. Can you identify the animals pictured and the phylum they are part of? Review the glossary for words you learned during the unit.

Now use your knowledge of invertebrates to answer each clue on the cards. Write your answer on the blank line at the bottom of each card. After you have answered all of the questions, check your answers. Correct any errors you may have made.

Now play a game with the cards. Cut out the cards, then cut each card in half on the dotted line. Turn the cards face down and arrange them in a square of eight rows and eight columns. Turn one card over and read it to yourself. Then turn another card over. Do they match? You are looking for a question and its answer. If they are not a match, turn them back over and repeat with two new cards. Play close attention to where you place the cards--it may help you make a match!

The game is over when you have matched all the cards.

Activity 2: Invertebrate Organisms *(Online)*

What do you remember about the many invertebrates and their groups? Test your recall and observe some fantastic marine invertebrates on this website!

ASSESS
Unit Assessment: Classification of Invertebrates (*Online*)

You will complete an online assessment of the main objectives covered so far in this unit. Follow the instructions online. Your assessment will be scored by the computer.

LEARN
Activity 3. Optional: ZlugQuest Measurement (*Online*)

Classification of Invertebrates Review Cards

I am an echinoderm. My body has radial symmetry. In order to move, I pump water into my tube feet. What is on the outside of my body?

Answer: _____

You can find me only in the water. I have nostrils but no eyes. I move through the water by bending my body from side to side. What am I?

Answer: _____

I am a segmented worm. What makes me different from other worms?

Answer: _____

If you look at me, you'll see that my body is divided into segments with jointed legs. My body is protected by an exoskeleton. What am I?

Answer: _____

I have a soft body with a thick skin called a mantle covering me. I also have a foot for movement. What am I?

Answer: _____

I have tentacles coming from my body, and they have long, stinging cells on the end. What am I?

Answer: _____

I am a type of worm that can regenerate a damaged body part when it is injured. I also have eyespots. What am I?

Answer: _____

I am a sponge living deep in the ocean. I reproduce through budding. What else is common among sponges?

Answer: _____

Student Guide
Lesson 1: Electric Charges and Magnetic Poles

All of us have had contact with electricity. We come into a room and turn on a light. We use a flashlight. We see lightning bolts. We also have experience with magnetism--our refrigerators stay closed using magnets, and many motors are loaded with them. Learn how these two things--electricity and magnetism--are related.

You already know something about electricity--just turn on a light! No doubt you have played with magnets, too, and have picked up metal objects with them. But did you know that electricity and magnetism are related?

Lesson Objectives

- Recognize that objects with the same electrical charges repel and objects with different electrical charges attract.
- Describe the Earth's magnetic field and identify magnetic north and south.

PREPARE

Approximate lesson time is 60 minutes.

Materials

For the Student

- 📖 Electric Discoveries: Your Scientist Notebook
- 📖 Come Here! Go Away!

  bar magnets, pair

  fabric, wool cloth

  household item - clothes hanger

  balloon (2)

  string

Keywords and Pronunciation

atom : A tiny particle that is the fundamental building block of any substance. The properties of an atom determine the properties of an element made up of only those atoms.

electron : A tiny part of an atom with a negative electrical charge. In an atom, electrons form a cloud around the nucleus.

proton : A tiny part of the nucleus of an atom, which has a positive electrical charge. The number of protons determines the chemical properties of the atom.

LEARN
Activity 1: Opposites Attract *(Online)*

Activity 2: Electric Discoveries: Your Scientist Notebook *(Offline)*

Keep a Scientist Notebook of electricity facts and fun you discover, just like famous scientists do.

Activity 3: Come Here! Go Away! *(Offline)*

Things are forced together, or *attract,* when their electrical charges are different. Things are pushed away, or *repel,* when their electrical charges are the same. Demonstrate these shocking events.

Safety

Do not use magnets near the computer.

ASSESS

Lesson Assessment: Electric Charges and Magnetic Poles (*Online*)

You will complete an online assessment covering the main objectives of this lesson. Your assessment will be scored by the computer.

Name _____   Date _____

Electric Discoveries: Your Scientist Notebook

How important is it to keep records? Think about important scientific discoveries and inventions. What if no one kept careful records of the movements of planets? What if no one kept notes on different kinds of complex treatments for diseases? Good written records help scientists remember exactly what they did, and what happened, without change. They can compare new experiments and results with old ones, and look for important differences and patterns.

Later in this unit you will learn about an English scientist named Michael Faraday. Michael Faraday made important discoveries in magnetism and electricity. He found that when a magnetic field increases or decreases, it produces electricity - an important principle used to build motors and generators.

This fine scientist began life with very little schooling as the son of a blacksmith. He loved books, so he worked in a bookbinder's shop. This job gave him the chance to read many books including encyclopedias and science books, as well as stories. He loved how he could check what he read in a chemistry book by doing his own observations, and so, personally, found the facts to be true.

Faraday was so interested in chemistry, that one day he borrowed money from a brother to attend a series of lectures on chemistry. These lectures had been created to teach young men just like him - not well off, but interested in science. He enjoyed these lectures on science so much, that he decided to become a "natural philosopher" (scientist). Since he had taken very careful records of the lectures he attended, he used his skills to bind them into a wonderful book. Then he presented the book to the director of the science institute that had offered the lectures, and asked for a job. Faraday was hired as a general assistant and bottle-washer: his first job close to science! While doing these tasks, he took time to document his own remarkable experiments, including the invention

Electric Discoveries: Your Scientist Notebook

of the electric motor in 1821. He eventually became the director of that very institute where he first heard science lectures.

Faraday's story shows many reasons why taking notes and keeping records are important: he used his notes and records to show others what he had done, and what he was capable of doing. During the entire unit, you will keep a science record book of the electricity and magnetism activities and experiments you perform.

Section off a part of your science binder or staple special pages together so that you can take notes as Faraday did. Then write the title, "Electric Discoveries: My Scientist Notebook." After each activity in this unit, you will be prompted to write in your Scientist Notebook. After recording your thoughts throughout the next six lessons, you will compile and present your findings in your own science lecture.

Name _____   Date _____

Come Here! Go Away!

Rubbing two neutral objects causes electrons to move off one object and onto another.

* A negatively charged object has more negatively charged particles (electrons).
* A positively charged object has less negatively charged particles (less electrons).

Materials

Balloons, 2
String
Wool cloth
Bar magnets

Attracting

1. Tie the balloon to string and hang it in a place you can reach. (You may want to suspend it from a coat hanger).
2. Hold the cloth near the balloon.
3. Nothing happens. Why? They are both neutral.
4. Rub the balloon quickly with the cloth. You are rubbing electrons off the cloth and onto the balloon right at this moment!
5. Hold the cloth near the balloon. Write what you observe. _____

_____

_____

_____

Come Here! Go Away!

Draw the positive and negative charges on the balloon and cloth before and after you rubbed the balloon.

Key

+ means positive

- means negative

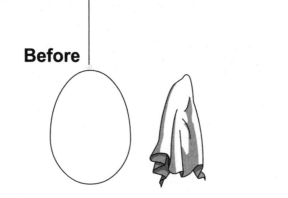

Before

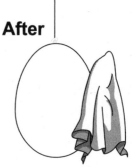

After

Repelling

1. Tie a new balloon to string and hang it near the first balloon.
2. Rub both balloons with the cloth.
3. Place the balloons near each other. Write what you observe. _____

_____

_____

Draw the charges on the balloons using the same key as before.

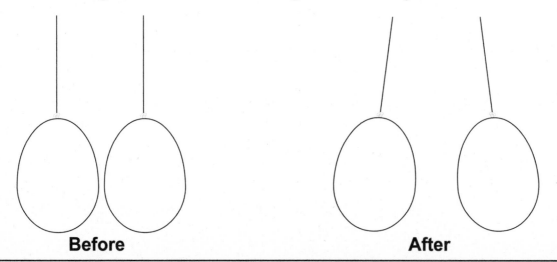

Before   **After**

Come Here! Go Away!

Magnetism

Magnets have poles always in pairs that repel and attract. Investigate repelling and attracting with the magnets by placing their ends near each other. Then, label the poles in the illustrations.

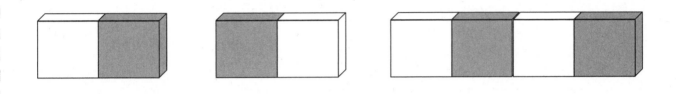

Repelling   **Attracting**

Key:

N = North pole

S = South pole

Your Scientist Notebook

On a separate piece of paper, make your first electricity and magnetism entry in your Scientist Notebook. Write the date so you have a record of your notes. Then make careful entries for your balloon experiments and your magnet experiments. Imagine someone else was going to read your notes and try to do the same experiments you did, to see if they get the same results.

Do you need to repeat your experiments in different ways to make sure you know what is happening? Draw any diagrams you may need in order to explain your findings.

Student Guide
Lesson 2: Magnet Madness

A magnet is a wonderful thing--especially when you start thinking about how it works. You know you can use a magnet to pick up many metal objects, but why? Explore how magnets work, and find out why scientists think the Earth acts like a giant magnet.

CAUTION: KEEP MAGNETS AWAY FROM YOUR COMPUTER.

Lesson Objectives

- Describe the Earth's magnetic field and identify magnetic north and south.
- Explain how to construct a temporary magnet.
- Explain that lightning is produced as a result of static discharge.

PREPARE

Approximate lesson time is 60 minutes.

Materials

For the Student

    🖳 Find Yourself

    bar magnets, pair

    household item - compass

    sewing needle

    bowl

    cardboard - float (foam, cork)

    water

Keywords and Pronunciation

atom : A tiny particle that is the fundamental building block of all substances. The properties of an atom determine the properties of an element made up only of those atoms.

aurora australis (uh-ROR-uh AW-struh-luhs)

aurora borealis (uh-ROR-uh bor-ee-A-luhs) : Lights seen at night in northern latitudes caused by electrically charged particles from the sun.

magnetic field : The magnetic effect every magnet creates in the space around it. The Earth has a very large magnetic field.

magnetic pole : A region of a magnet where the magnetic field is especially strong. All magnetic poles are either north or south poles. In a bar magnet, the poles are at the ends.

LEARN

Activity 1: Magnificent Magnets *(Online)*

Activity 2: Mapping with Magnets *(Offline)*

The world is a pretty big place, and if you don't know your way around you'll soon get lost. Make a temporary magnet and a tool that, for centuries, has been helping people find their way. Remember, stay far away from the computer when you work with magnets!

Activity 3: Scientist Notebook *(Offline)*

Today you made important "discoveries" about magnetism. As you know, it is important for scientists to keep records of their discoveries and investigations. Write about your discoveries in your notebook. Include the following:

- The date and time
- What you discovered as you made the compass and what you can use it for
- What happened to the needle as you magnetized it
- Any surprises that came up during the lesson

Make your notes clear enough that someone else finding them could do the same thing you did, and compare results with your results.

Use an index card to make a compass card. Write the north, south, east, and west on the card in their proper locations. Use your tool to find the following and record them in your notebook.

1. The direction the sun rises
2. The direction the sun sets
3. A building north of you
4. An organism south of you
5. Any object of your choice and its direction

Keep track of the entries you are making in your Scientist Notebook. You will need them at the end of the unit.

ASSESS

Lesson Assessment: Magnet Madness *(Offline)*

You will complete an offline assessment covering the main objectives of this lesson. Your learning coach will score this assessment.

Name _____ Date _____

Find Yourself

Exploring magnetism is fun, and so is using magnetism to explore!
With a few simple tools, you can make a magnet that you can use
as a compass. It's the same idea that ocean mariners and desert
explorers have used for centuries.

A *compass* is a tool people use to figure out direction. It uses the
Earth's magnetic north pole. Here's how it works:

- First, hold the compass in front of you. A compass has an N, S,
  W, and E for the four cardinal directions.
- Then, watch where the pointer stops.
- The pointer lines up with the Earth's
  magnetic field, with one side (the north
  side) attracted to the magnetic north
  pole.
- To align the compass, turn the compass
  body until the pointer is directly over the
  N. Label N on the paper.
- Once you know north, you can then
  figure out south, west, and east—or
  northeast or southwest or…

**This way
is north.**

Materials
needle
a float (cork, foam meat tray, cardboard)
bowl – not metal
water
bar magnet
tape

Find Yourself

WARNING: Before working with magnets move far away from the computer. Use caution when working with the needle.

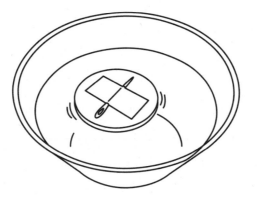

Procedure:

1. Fill the bowl with water to make your compass case. Glass or plastic bowls work best.
2. Make a float. A *float* is a small, flat piece of lightweight material that will float on water. Cardboard will work for a while, but cork or a piece of a foam meat tray is best.
3. Next, make a magnet. Put the needle flat on the bar magnet, with one end facing the N pole of the bar magnet, and the other facing the S pole. Now pull the needle by the end so it slides along its length from S pole to N pole, and repeat several times. Always pull in the same direction to keep from mixing up the magnetic poles.
4. Test your needle for magnetism—try sticking one end to the refrigerator or attracting other needles.
5. Once your needle is magnetized, attach it to the float with tape.

Troubleshooting:

- Other metals can interfere with your compass.
- If your container is too small or your float too large, your compass will be drawn to the side. Find a larger container.

Find Yourself

1. Place your compass in the water with the needle side up. Let it settle down. What happens? Try turning the float around, and then gently turn the bowl. _____

   _____

   _____

2. Explain how the needle became magnetic. Mention electrons in your answer. _____

   _____

   _____

Name _____   Date _____

Magnet Madness Assessment

1. Tell how to make a temporary magnet using electricity. _____

   _____

   _____

   _____

2. Tell how to make a temporary magnet without electricity. _____

   _____

   _____

   _____

3. Describe what happens to electrons in an iron object when the
   object is magnetized. _____

   _____

   _____

   _____

   _____

4. Tell what scientists think makes Earth a magnet. _____

   _____

   _____

   _____

   _____

Magnet Madness Assessment

5. Draw lines to show the Earth's magnetic field. Label the approximate locations of the magnetic north and south poles.

Student Guide
Lesson 3: Static Electricity - Truly Shocking

It's a bit of shock to touch a doorknob and get...well...a shock. Why does this happen? Find out more about static electricity and learn how a charge is built up and how a charge is discharged.

Lesson Objectives

- Explain that friction can build up static electrical charges when two objects are rubbed together and transfer electrons from one surface to the other.
- Recognize that *static electricity* is the buildup of electrical charges on an object.
- Explain that lightning is produced as a result of static discharge.
- Recognize that *electric current* is the flow of electrons through a wire.

PREPARE

Approximate lesson time is 60 minutes.

Materials

For the Student

   🖥 Action Static

    household item - comb

    household item - puffed rice

    household item - wool sweater or cloth

    balloon

    water - (sink)

   🖥 Get a Charge from an Electroscope

    jar - glass

    index cards, 4" x 6"

    paper clip - large

Keywords and Pronunciation

conduction : The application of an electric charge to an object by direct contact with a charged object. The glass rod got its electric charge by conduction.

friction : Rubbing two objects together to create an imbalance of charges. Friction was part of the reason I got shocked when I touched the doorknob.

induction : The application of an electric charge to an object through the nearness of a charged object. The glass globe got its electric charge by induction.

static electricity : Electricity on the surface of objects, better thought of as unbalanced-charge electricity. Lightning is the huge discharge of static electricity charge from a cloud.

LEARN
Activity 1: More Than Just a Shock *(Online)*

Activity 2: Action Static *(Offline)*
Understanding static electricity will help you understand what goes on behind the scenes of what may seem like tricks. See how static works in interesting ways, then make notes of what you see in your Scientist Notebook.

Activity 3: Electroscope *(Online)*
An electroscope is a cool tool for studying electricity. It works with conduction of charges from one object to another.

ASSESS
Lesson Assessment: Static Electricity - Truly Shocking (*Offline*)
You will complete an offline assessment covering the main objectives of this lesson. Your learning coach will score this assessment.

Name _____ Date _____

Action Static

What are some examples of static electricity?

1. _____

2. _____

3. _____

One way to produce static electricity is with friction. When you rub two things together, friction causes electrons to move from one object to another. The object that gains electrons becomes negatively charged. The object that loses electrons becomes positively charged. With these unbalanced charges, you can observe interesting effects. Some people may believe they are tricks, but there's real science behind them that you should know.

Materials
        wool sweater or cloth
        balloon
        puffed rice cereal
        comb
        water (sink)

Part 1: The Comb and Water Trick

1. Turn on a water faucet and allow a thin stream of water to flow.
2. Charge the comb by rubbing it many times with the wool cloth.
3. Hold the comb close to the stream.

Make notes about what you see happening in your Science Notebook.

Action Static

Part 2: The Puffed Rice in a Balloon Trick

1. Put 5-10 pieces of puffed-rice cereal into a deflated balloon.
2. Inflate the balloon and tie it closed.
3. Hold the balloon with one hand so that the mouth of the balloon is against your body.
4. Charge the balloon by stroking it 20-25 times with the piece of wool cloth.
5. Hold the balloon by the mouth so it hangs down freely.
6. If needed, give the balloon a little thump to get the puffed rice to the bottom of the balloon.
7. Slowly move your finger toward the cereal until your finger touches the balloon.
8. Rub the palm of your hand over the entire lower part of the balloon.

Make notes in your Science Notebook about what you see happening. Think about what types of charges attract and repel. Make sure someone else could repeat what you did from reading your notes.

Part 3: Science Notebook

Consider what you saw today in your activities. In your Science Notebook, explain why they are not tricks. Tell what happened to the objects that made them behave the way they did. Note any surprises or unexplained phenomena. Did you try your own tests after these two? What did you notice then? Don't forget to date your notes.

Explain your notes to an adult to check your work.

Name _____   Date _____

Get a Charge from an Electroscope

This time, take a backward approach to learn about a cool science tool. Make an electroscope first, try some tests, then see if you can figure out what happened.

Materials
balloon
paper clip - large
aluminum foil
tape
scissors
wool sweater or cloth
glass jar
index card

Procedure
1. Unfold the paper clip and stick it through an index card.
2. Refold the paper clip so it looks like an S.
3. Take a long, thin strip of aluminum foil and wrap the middle once or twice around the bottom part of the S. The two sides of the strip should be equal and should hang down, not touching but very close together.
4. Place the index card on the top of the jar and tape it to the rim. The foil strips should be inside the jar and the top of the paper clip should be outside. This is your electroscope.
5. Charge a balloon by rubbing it with a wool cloth in the same direction 25-30 times.
6. Bring the balloon close to the paper clip outside the jar.

Get a Charge from an Electroscope

What happened?
You should see the foil strips separate.

Why?
When you touch the charged balloon to the electroscope, negative charges are transferred to the wire. What type of static buildup occurs when one charged object touches another object? _____

_____.

The buildup of negative charges travels down the wire to the foil strips. The strips are overloaded with negative charges. Lots of negative charges are lots of similar charges, and you know what happens to similar charges…they repel!

Science Notebook
Sketch and label an electroscope in your notebook. Draw a diagram showing how negative charges are transferred from the balloon to the wire, and then to the aluminum strips. Use plus signs for positive charges and minus signs for negative charges. Date your work.

Share your diagram with an adult to check your work.

Name _____   Date _____

Lesson Assessment

Circle the correct answers.

1. The buildup of electric charges on an object is known as:
   A. friction
   B. magnetism
   C. static electricity
   D. dangerous

2. Describe how friction can cause a buildup of electrical charges.
   In your answer name two objects from the list.

       your hand
       glass
       your hair
       nylon
       wool
       fur
       silk
       paper
       cotton
       hard rubber
       polyester

   _____
   _____
   _____
   _____

3. How are lightning and a shock from static electricity related to
   each other? _____

   _____
   _____
   _____
   _____

Student Guide
Lesson 4: Electric Currents

The electricity you are most familiar with is the kind that comes to your house through wires. How does this kind of electricity differ from static electricity? In what ways is it similar? Find out about electric currents and how electrons can flow through wires.

Lesson Objectives

- Identify the parts of a circuit: battery, light, wire, and switch.
- Differentiate between a *series circuit* and a *parallel circuit*.
- Recognize that *electric current* is the flow of electrons through a wire.
- State that electric currents flow easily through materials that are conductors and do not flow easily through materials that are insulators.

PREPARE

Approximate lesson time is 60 minutes.

Advance Preparation

- One site you may use to purchase the 4.5v battery is www.campmor.com. If you choose not to purchase one, 2 D size batteries will work for the experiment in lieu of the 4.5v battery. Make sure you place them with positive and negative ends facing each other.
- Save the completed circuit for use in the next lesson.

Materials

For the Student
    🖥 Build a Circuit
       electrical tape
       electrical wire, plastic coated - 2 feet
       light bulb holders (3)
       light bulbs, miniature (5)
       battery - 4.5 V (D cell can work)
       brads (2)
       cardboard
       knife
       paper clip
       scissors

🖥 Make an Electric Quiz Board

  hole punch

  light bulb - small

  light bulb holder

  wire, copper - 3 meters

  battery - D cell or 4.5 volt

  cardboard - sturdy, 33 cm x 30 cm

  crayons 8 - for decorating (optional)

  paper clips - metal (14)

  tape, masking

Keywords and Pronunciation

electric current : The flow of electrons through a wire.

LEARN
Activity 1: Electric Currents *(Online)*

Activity 2: Build a Circuit *(Offline)*

Investigate the flow of electric current by building two types of circuits. Remove parts of the circuits to see the effects.

Safety

The bulbs may be hot. Use a cloth or oven mitt to unscrew them.

ASSESS

Lesson Assessment: Electric Currents (*Offline*)

You will complete an offline assessment covering the main objectives of this lesson. Your learning coach will score this assessment.

LEARN
Activity 3. Optional: Make an Electric Quiz Board *(Offline)*

From what you've learned, you can build a quiz board that you can use with your friends. Test them on their electricity knowledge! Have your friends compete for prizes.

Name _____   Date _____

Build a Circuit

How are parallel and series circuits different? Construct both types to investigate. Record your observations in your Scientist Notebook.

Materials
4.5-volt battery
small bulbs, 4
bulb holders, 2
paper clip
electrical tape
copper wire, 60 cm
   – cut into 4 pieces and strip the ends
cardboard
brass fasteners, 2
scissors
knife

Wind bare end of wire underneath head of screw and tighten screw head down.

Lab Safety:
The bulbs may be hot. Use a cloth or oven mitt to unscrew them.

Procedure
1. Join the battery, bulbs, and wires in a series circuit as shown. Use electrical tape to attach the wires to the battery.
2. Push one paper fastener through cardboard. Hook a paper clip to the second fastener and push this fastener through the cardboard.
3. Turn the cardboard over. Wrap one wire around each paper fastener. Tape down the legs of the fastener.
4. Press the paper clip onto the free paper fastener. Electricity should flow.

Build a Circuit

Series circuit
Use your switch to turn the lights on.
While both bulbs are lit, unscrew one of
the bulbs. Record your observations in
your Scientist Notebook.

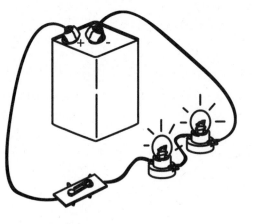

Parallel circuit
Set up a parallel circuit as shown. While
both bulbs are lit, unscrew one of the
bulbs. Record your observations in your
Scientist Notebook.

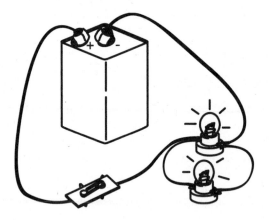

Scientist Notebook
Answer the following questions in your Scientist Notebook.
1. How do you know your circuits were complete?
2. Compare the brightness of the bulbs in the series circuit to the bulbs
   in the parallel circuit.
3. Compare the effect of unscrewing the bulbs in a series circuit to the
   bulbs in the parallel circuit.
4. How is the flow of electricity different in a series circuit and a parallel
   circuit?
5. Some older types of holiday lights would not work if even one bulb
   burned out. What kind of circuit was this? How were lights improved
   by changing the kind of circuit?

Share your answers with an adult to check them.

Name _____   Date _____

Lesson Assessment

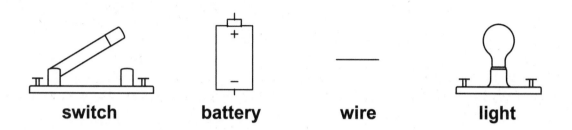

switch   **battery**   **wire**   **light**

1. Draw a series circuit. You may refer to the icons above to help you sketch each part.

2. Draw a parallel circuit. You may refer to the icons above to help you sketch each part.

Lesson Assessment

3. What happens if a bulb is removed from a series circuit? Why? _____

_____

_____

_____

4. What happens if you remove a bulb from a parallel circuit? Why? _____

_____

_____

_____

_____

5. To produce an electric current, you need a continuous source of _____.
   A. electrons
   B. protons
   C. watts
   D. static

Name _____ Date _____

Make an Electric Quiz Board

Have an adult help you follow the directions to make an electric quiz board that lights up when someone knows the right answer.

Materials
Cardboard, sturdy – 33 cm tall x 30 cm wide
Hole punch
Light bulb
Bulb holder
Battery – D-cell or 4.5 volt
Brass fasteners, 12
Metal paper clips, 14
Copper wire, 3 m
Scissors
Masking tape
Electrical tape
Crayons for decorating (optional)

Procedure
1. Punch six holes down each side of the cardboard, about 2 cm from the edges.
2. Slip a brass fastener through each hole and bend over the ends on the back.
3. Cut the wire into six 35 cm pieces, two 45 cm pieces, and one 17 cm piece. If the wire is insulated, strip the ends of insulation.
4. Wrap the bare end of each medium length wire to a paper clip so it makes a good contact. These wires will connect your questions and correct answer (or answers).

Make an Electric Quiz Board

5. Use the longest wires for the front of the board. Add a paper clip to the end of each long wire. Connect the bare end of one wire to a D-cell battery with tape.
6. Connect the bare end of the other long wire to the bulb holder.
7. Use the shortest wire to connect the other end of the battery to the other bulb holder connection.
8. Write a multiple-choice question. Cut the question and the answers apart. Tape them next to a brass fastener "button" on the front of the board.
9. Hang one medium-sized connector paperclip on the question. Hang the other on the answer. Connect the two wires.
10. Test your quiz board. Touch one of the paper clips on the long wire to the question and the other paper clip on the long wire to the answer.

Does the light bulb light up? If not, check all your connections to see they are secure and try again. Double check all your questions and answers to see that you have wired them correctly. When you get it to work, can you explain what's making your Electric Quiz Board work?

Each group will need six 16-inch pieces, two 20-inch pieces and one 8-inch piece of wire with all ends stripped of insulation.

Student Guide
Lesson 5: Resistance, Conductors, Insulators

The materials that make up a circuit play an important part in the flow of electrical charges through a circuit. You will learn that a charge travels easier through some materials than others. For example, in some materials, electrical charges cannot flow at all. These materials can help make the use of electricity safer.

Lesson Objectives

- State that electric currents flow easily through materials that are conductors and do not flow easily through materials that are insulators.
- Give examples of conductors and insulators.
- Describe how certain materials affect the flow of electricity through a wire.
- State that electric current produces magnetic fields and that an electromagnet can be made by wrapping a wire around a piece of iron and then running electricity through the wire.

PREPARE

Approximate lesson time is 60 minutes.

Advance Preparation

- You will need to save your circuit set-up for the next lesson. For the Fruity Electricity activity, you can purchase a copper screw and zinc screw at a home repair center.

Materials

For the Student

🖥 Conductors and Insulators

coin

drinking glass

household item - 2 ft - covered wire

household item - 4.5 volt battery

household item - bulb holder

household item - small lightbulb

plastic

rubber band

aluminum foil

paper clip

paper, notebook

pencil

tape, clear

household item - 1 copper screw about 5 cm

household item - 1 holiday light

household item - 1 zinc screw about 5 cm

household item - lemon

Keywords and Pronunciation

conductor : Any material through which electricity can flow. A copper wire is a good conductor of electric charge as it flows through the circuit.

insulator : A substance that cannot conduct electricity very well. The rubber casing around the speaker wire serves as an insulator for the electrical current.

resistance : A measure of how strongly a substance opposes the flow of electricity. The unit of resistance in an electric circuit is the ohm.

LEARN
Activity 1: More About Circuits *(Online)*

Activity 2: Conductors and Insulators *(Offline)*

You already know how to create an electrical circuit using wire and a battery. Now add new materials to the circuit to see what effect they have on the bulb in the circuit. Will the bulb light up?

Caution: Bulbs may get hot.

Safety

Bulbs may get hot.

ASSESS
Lesson Assessment: Resistance, Conductors, Insulators (*Online*)

You will complete an online assessment covering the main objectives of this lesson. Your assessment will be scored by the computer.

LEARN
Activity 3. Optional: Fruity Electricity *(Online)*

Can fruit help make electricity? Experiment with a fruit you can find in the grocery store--a lemon!

Go to the next screen to get started.

Name _____   Date _____

Conductors and Insulators

The circuit you created uses a battery, a copper wire, a switch, and a bulb. When the circuit is closed, the bulb will light up.

Hypothesis:

Using the same circuit, what do you predict will happen when you add any of the following materials as a part of the circuit?

Materials	Will the material complete the circuit and light the bulb?
Aluminum foil	
Drinking glass	
Paper clip	
Coin	
Pencil	
Paper	
Rubber band	

Materials:

completed circuit

aluminum foil

drinking glass

paper clip

coin

pencil

paper

rubberband

Conductors and Insulators

Lab Safety:

Do not touch the bulbs. They may be hot.

Procedure:

1. Remove the switch from the circuit. Do not attach the two ends of wire.
2. Place a piece of aluminum foil between the two ends of wire. Touch both ends of the wire to the aluminum foil.
3. Does this action complete the circuit and light the bulb? Record your observations in the table below.
4. Repeat the procedure using the remaining items in the table instead of aluminum foil.

Observations/Analysis:

Materials	Did the material complete the circuit and light the bulb?
Aluminum foil	
Drinking glass	
Paper clip	
Coin	
Pencil	
Paper	
Rubber band	

Science Notebook:

What conclusions can you draw about the materials completed the circuit and lit the bulb? What about the materials that did not light the bulb? _____

_____

_____

_____

_____

Student Guide
Lesson 6: Electromagnetism

In this lesson you will learn more about the relationship between electricity and magnetism. You will also see how a doorbell works and understand electric generators and motors.

KEEP MAGNETS AWAY FROM COMPUTER AT ALL TIMES.

Lesson Objectives

- State that electric current produces magnetic fields and that an electromagnet can be made by wrapping a wire around a piece of iron and then running electricity through the wire.
- Recognize that electromagnets are used in electric motors, generators, and other devices, such as doorbells and earphones.
- Describe how to increase or decrease the strength of an electromagnet.

PREPARE

Approximate lesson time is 60 minutes.

Advance Preparation

- You will need to save your copper wire for the electromagnet investigation in this lesson.

- One site you may use to purchase the 4.5v battery is www.campmor.com. If you choose not to purchase one, 2 D size batteries will work for the experiment in lieu of the 4.5v battery. Make sure you place them with positive and negative ends facing each other.

Materials

For the Student

    🖥 The Strongest Electromagnet

      battery - 4.5 volt

      copper wire

      nail, iron - not rusty

      paper clip - 20

Keywords and Pronunciation

electromagnet : A temporary magnet made using electric current, usually running around a metal core.

Hans Christian Oersted (hahns KREES-tyahn OUR-sted)

LEARN
Activity 1: Electromagnetism *(Online)*

Activity 2: The Strongest Electromagnet *(Offline)*

Annabelle and Simon were two students who decided to make an electromagnet. They found that one electromagnet was stronger than the other. Why were their electromagnets so different if they were made the same way? Make an electromagnet to find out.

Safety

Move well away from the computer and any wet area before doing this experiment.

ASSESS

Lesson Assessment: Electromagnetism (*Offline*)

You will complete an offline assessment covering the main objectives of this lesson. Your learning coach will score this assessment.

LEARN

Activity 3. Optional: Electrical Safety (*Online*)

Just as important as knowing about electricity is knowing about electrical safety. How electricity safety savvy are you?

<u>Name</u>_____ <u>Date</u>_____

The Strongest Electromagnet

The circuit you created uses a battery, a copper wire, a switch, and a bulb. When the circuit is closed, the bulb will light up.

Using wire, an iron core, and a battery to make an electromagnet is a simple way to see the relationship between electricity and magnetism. Some electromagnets are stronger than others. Investigate two ways you can change the strength of an electromagnet.

The Story:
Annabelle and Simon had just learned about electromagnets. They both decided to build electromagnets to see who could make the strongest one.

They both found clean iron nails, not rusty old ones. They both wrapped their nails with copper wire, in tight coils. They both attached one end of the wire to the positive end of a 4.5 volt battery and the other end of the wire to the negative end. Then, Annabelle and Simon attempted to pick up paper clips with their electromagnets.

Annabelle's electromagnet picked up more paper clips than Simon's. Her electromagnet was stronger. They examined both electromagnets to see what could have made the difference. After observing the two magnets for a while they had an idea. They tried their idea in a new experiment. They wanted to find out if wrapping the wire more times around the nail made an electromagnet stronger.

Hypothesis:
Predict whether or not more coils will make an electromagnet stronger.

Give a reason for your prediction. _____

_____

_____

_____

The Strongest Electromagnet

Materials
battery – 4.5 volt
iron nail – not rusty
paper clips
copper wire

Procedure:
1. Wrap the iron nail with the copper wire 10 times. Make your coils tight.
2. Attach one end of the wire to the positive end of the battery. Attach the other end to the negative end.
3. Hold your electromagnet over a pile of paper clips and try to pick some up.
4. Repeat steps 1–3 two more times making 20 coils and then 30 coils.

Circle what you change in the experiment (independent variable). Underline what will happen because of the change (dependent variable).

kind of nail	voltage of battery	number of coils
kind of wire	strength of magnetism	kind of paper clips

Observations

Number of coils	Number of paper clips
10	
20	
30	

The Strongest Electromagnet

Analysis

Make a bar graph to show how the strength of the electromagnet changed during each try.

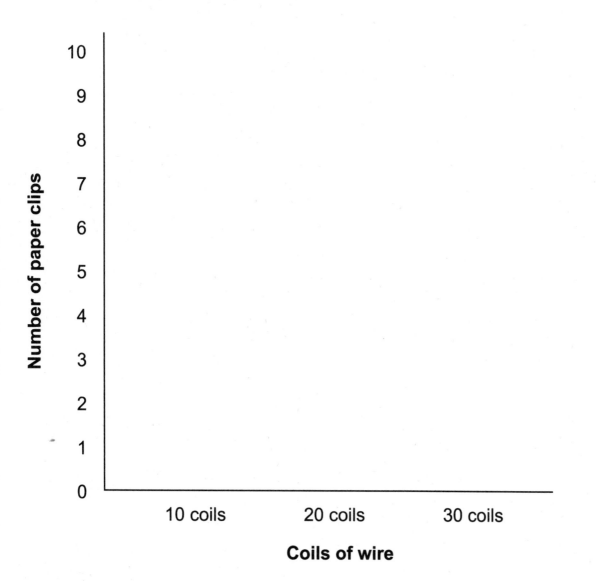

Conclusion

In your Scientist Notebook, describe the test you conducted today. Answer these questions:

1. What is the likely reason that Annabelle's magnet was stronger? Can you think of another reason Annabelle's magnet might be stronger? Describe an experiment you might do to test that idea.

Name _____ Date _____

Electromagnetism Assessment

1. If you wrap a wire around a piece of iron, and then run electricity through the wire, what happens to the iron? _____

   _____

   _____

   _____

2. Read this data from an experiment. Then state which electromagnet was wrapped with the most coils. _____

   Electromagnet Tests:
   Laura's electromagnet: 12 paper clips
   Rachel's electromagnet: 5 paper clips
   Ethan's electromagnet: 7 paper clips

3. Circle the objects that use an electromagnet.

   Motor   Doorbell   Scissors   Earphones

   Bicycle gears   Generator   Mechanical pencil

4. Electromagnets are used at junk yards to lift and move giant pieces of metal from one place to another. What happens to the magnetism and the huge pieces of metal as soon as the electricity is switched off?

   _____

   _____

   _____

Student Guide
Lesson 7: Unit Review and Assessment

Flip your light switch to "on" as you review the unit and take the unit assessment. Present all of the findings you made during your investigation of electricity and magnetism.

Lesson Objectives

- Recognize that objects with the same electrical charges repel and objects with different electrical charges attract.
- Explain how to construct a temporary magnet.
- Explain that friction can build up static electrical charges when two objects are rubbed together and transfer electrons from one surface to the other.
- Identify the parts of a circuit: battery, light, wire, and switch.
- State that electric currents flow easily through materials that are conductors and do not flow easily through materials that are insulators.
- Recognize that electromagnets are used in electric motors, generators, and other devices, such as doorbells and earphones.
- Demonstrate that magnets have two poles (north and south) and that like poles repel each other while unlike poles attract each other.
- State that electric currents produce magnetic fields and that an electromagnet can be made by wrapping a wire around a piece of iron and then running electricity through the wire.
- Differentiate between series and parallel circuits.
- Describe the earth's magnetic field and identify magnetic north and south.
- Describe the Earth's magnetic field and identify magnetic north and south.
- Demonstrate mastery of the important knowledge and skills of this unit.
- Differentiate between a *series circuit* and a *parallel circuit*.
- State that electric current produces magnetic fields and that an electromagnet can be made by wrapping a wire around a piece of iron and then running electricity through the wire.

PREPARE

Approximate lesson time is 60 minutes.

Materials

For the Student

🖳 Posters and Presenting: Be A Modern Day Faraday

household item - assorted art supplies

tape, adhesive

cardboard - or posterboard

markers

paper, construction, 9" x 12"

paper, notebook

LEARN
Activity 1: Electric Obstacle Course (Online)

Activity 2: Be a Modern Day Faraday (Offline)

Good scientists notice details about their experiments. Great scientists write them down. Even better scientists make a poster! Share some things you discovered while being a super scientist during this unit.

ASSESS
Unit Assessment: Electricity and Magnetism (Online)

Complete an offline Unit Assessment. Your learning coach will score this part of the Assessment.

LEARN
Activity 3. Optional: ZlugQuest Measurement (Online)

Name _____   Date _____

Posters and Presenting: Be A Modern Day Faraday

During this unit on electricity and magnetism, you have been keeping notes in your scientist notebook. You started this after reading about Michael Faraday, an English scientist who kept careful notes about experiments because he knew it would help make him a smarter person.

Michael Faraday enjoyed sharing his notes with others. He always talked to his discussion group about electricity.

Share what you have learned about electricity and magnetism with an adult. Make a poster about what you have studied:

- Static
- Magnets
- Electric currents and circuits
- Conductors and insulators
- Electromagnets

On your poster, include a fact and picture about each topic in the list. You might even include something surprising you found out during your experiments. Use a large enough piece of paper or poster board (you can tape smaller pieces together). Write large so people can read your poster.

Give your presentation a catchy title. When you present your poster, be sure to tell WHAT you studied, WHEN, and HOW. Tell where people can get in touch with you after your presentation.

Name _____   Date _____

Electricity and Magnetism Assessment

Circle the correct answer.

1. Two objects are rubbed together, creating friction. What will likely happen next?
   A. Protons will be rubbed from one surface to another.
   B. Electrons will be rubbed from one surface to another.
   C. A flow of electricity will start.
   D. The two objects will cool down.

2. Electric current flows easily through a _____.
   A. charger
   B. resistance
   C. volts
   D. conductor

3. You can make an iron nail magnetic by wrapping it in wire and sending electricity through the wire.
   A. True
   B. False

Use the words in the Word Bank to fill in the blanks. You may not need to use all of the words.

protons	neutrons	electrons	switch
battery	wire	light	iron core
insulator	resistance		

4. When an object is negatively charged, it has more _____ than _____.

5. You can make a simple series circuit by connecting a _____, _____, _____, and _____.

6. An _____ is a material through which electricity does not flow freely.

Electricity and Magnetism Assessment

7. Draw charges on the balloons to show them attracting.

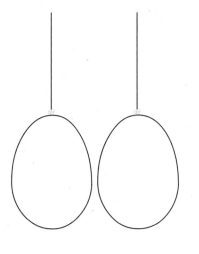

8. Draw charges on the balloons to show them repelling.

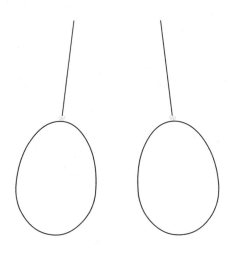

Electricity and Magnetism Assessment

9. Draw two sets of bar magnets. Show one pair attracting. Show one pair repelling. Label the north and south poles correctly.

10. Draw lines to show the Earth's magnetic field. Label the location of the magnetic north and south poles.

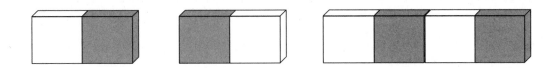

11. A needle rubbed with a magnet becomes magnetic. Is this a temporary or permanent magnet? _____

12. What do scientists think makes Earth a giant magnet? _____

_____

_____

_____

Electricity and Magnetism Assessment

13. Label the battery, switch, lamp, and wire in each circuit below.

Series Circuit   **Parallel Circuit**

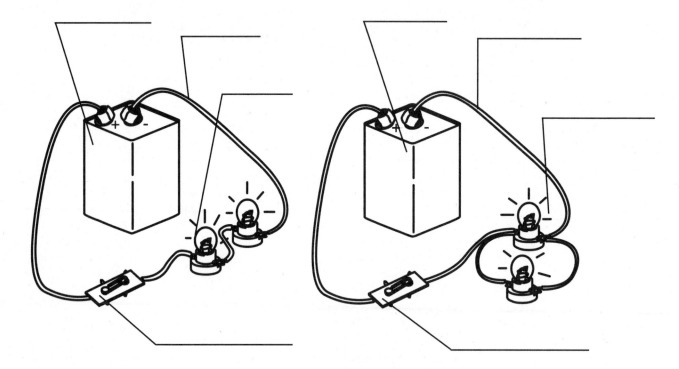

14. What would happen to the other light if you removed
    one of the bulbs from a series circuit? Explain. _____

    _____

    _____

15. What would happen to the other light if you removed
    one of the bulbs from a parallel circuit? Explain. _____

    _____

    _____

16. Name two devices that use electromagnets. _____

    _____

    _____

Student Guide
Lesson 1: Rocks and Minerals

A simple rock might not look like much. Look closer, however, and you will see that it is formed from smaller substances--minerals. Where do minerals come from? What are they made of? Discover the answers to these questions, and learn how the birth of rocks is related to two awesome phenomena in nature--volcanoes and earthquakes.

Minerals and rocks are only part of the materials that make up the Earth. From its solid metallic core to the pebbles scattered on a beach, the Earth is a complex mixture of layers and materials.

Lesson Objectives

- Identify the four main layers of the Earth and describe their characteristics.
- Explain that rock is composed of different combinations of minerals.

PREPARE

Approximate lesson time is 60 minutes.

Advance Preparation

- In this Science activity, your student will be using the rock kit for the first time. For the first few lessons in this unit she should not know the identity of the different rocks and minerals. Remove the lid with the key from the box, and set it aside for later reference.

Materials

For the Student

- Rock Samples

  K12 Rocks and Minerals Kit

  magnifying glass

  paper, notebook

  pencil

Keywords and Pronunciation

Andriji Mohorovicic (ahn-DREE-yah maw-hawr-oh-VEE-chech)

crust : Earth's hard, rocky covering. The crust is the outermost layer of the Earth.

crystal : A solid substance whose atoms are arranged in repeating patterns. Crystals can be very beautiful, often looking like jewels.

galena (guh-LEE-nuh)

igneous (IG-nee-uhs) : A class of rocks that forms from magma and lava. Obsidian may look like black glass but, in fact, it is a kind of igneous rock.

inner core : The center of Earth. Scientists think it is made of solid iron and nickel. The inner core has 30 times more mass than the moon.

mantle : the part of earth that is beneath the crust and is made up of rock; about 84 percent of the earth´s volume is in the mantle

---

metamorphic (meh-tuh-MOR-fik) : A class of rocks that forms when heat and pressure act on igneous or sedimentary rock.

mineral : A nonliving substance that is made up of crystals and is found in nature. The Earth's crust contains many minerals.

outer core : The part of Earth that is beneath the mantle and contains melted iron and nickel. The outer core surrounds the inner core.

rock : A hard material made up of two or more minerals. There are three categories of rocks in the Earth.

LEARN
Activity 1: The Stuff of the Earth (Online)

Activity 2: Rock Sampling (Offline)
It's time to become a Rock Explorer! Look inside your rock kit to see samples of different rocks and minerals. Explore the samples and use a magnifying glass to find what characteristics they may have in common.

ASSESS
Lesson Assessment: Rocks and Minerals (Offline)
You will complete an offline assessment covering the main objectives of this lesson. Your learning coach will score this assessment.

LEARN
Activity 3. Optional: Nearby Rocks (Online)
Diamonds are found only in certain places around the world. Do you think there are diamonds near your house? Visit a website to see what types of rocks and minerals are mined where you live.

Name _____   Date _____

Rock Samples

Are you ready to explore your rock kit? It contains both rocks and minerals, and they all have different characteristics. Take some time to look at each sample. How does each one feel? What colors can you see? If you use a magnifying glass can you see any crystals?

Place all the samples on a table. Separate the dark samples from the light samples, and use the numbers on the rocks to fill in the chart below. Then re-classify the samples looking for the rest of the characteristics listed on the chart.

Characteristics	Rock Numbers
Dark in color	
Light in color	
Visible crystals	
No visible crystals	
Visibly different minerals	
No visibly different minerals	
No visibly different minerals with visible crystals	
No visibly different minerals with no visible crystals	

Name _____ Date _____

Rocks and Minerals Assessment

Use the words in the Word Bank to label the different layers of the Earth and to fill in the blanks. You may use some words more than once or not at all.

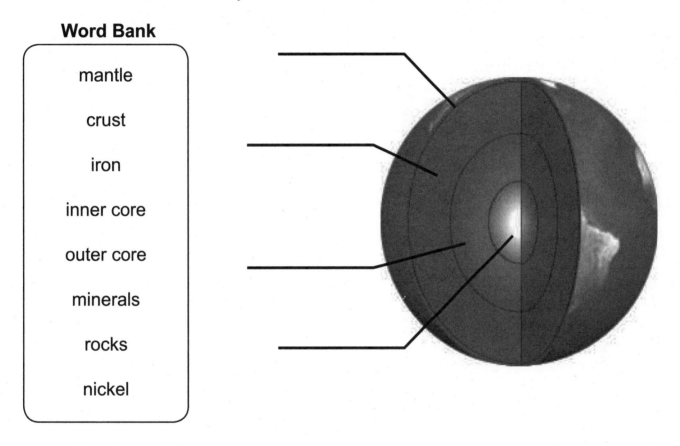

Word Bank

mantle

crust

iron

inner core

outer core

minerals

rocks

nickel

1. The thin, hard, rocky outer layer is called the _____ .

2. The extremely hot layer that is made almost entirely of solid iron is the _____ .

3. _____ are made up of two or more _____ .

4. The _____ is between the outer core and the crust. It is made of solid rock, but is under so much pressure that it is constantly moving.

5. The _____ is made mostly of liquid iron.

Student Guide
Lesson 2: Crystal Shapes

Crystals are some of the most beautiful of nature's creations. The faint reflection from a ruby or emerald is a wonderful thing to behold. What are crystals, though, and why do they sparkle and gleam the way they do? You'll find that the arrangement of their atoms or molecules holds the key to understanding crystals.

Lesson Objectives

- Describe two types of crystal structures--cubic and hexagonal.
- Explain that the size of a crystal depends on the rate at which it was cooled.

PREPARE

Approximate lesson time is 60 minutes.

Advance Preparation

- In this science lesson, your student will be using the rock kit for the second time. For the first few lessons in this unit, we don't want her to know the identity of the different rocks and minerals. Remove the lid with the key from the box, and set it aside for later reference.
- Your student will need at least four days for crystals to grow in the "Cool" Crystals activity. Start the investigation early, or start it during the lesson and return to it later.

Materials

For the Student

 📖 Crystal Shapes
 📖 "Cool" Crystals
 jar - baby food/plastic cups (2)
 oven mitt
 salt - Epsom
 heat source
 magnifying glass
 pipe cleaners
 pot
 ruler
 safety goggles
 spoon
 water

Keywords and Pronunciation

crystal : A substance, often made of a single compound or element, that forms in a regular repeating pattern as rocks cool. I found a quartz crystal inside a granite rock.

cubic : A type of crystal structure formed from stacks of four-sided shapes (cubes). The crystal structure of gold is cubic.

hexagonal : A type of crystal structure formed from six-sided shapes. Ice has a hexagonal crystal structure.

LEARN
Activity 1: Amazing Crystals *(Online)*

Activity 2: Crystal Shapes *(Offline)*

Do you know what *orderly* means? A room with clothing folded and put away and trash emptied is orderly. Rocks contain orderly parts called *crystals.* Crystals form in regular patterns over and over again. Explore two types of crystal patterns.

Activity 3: "Cool" Crystals *(Offline)*

Crystals form in different patterns but also in different sizes. Find out the effect of how fast a crystal cools on its size.

Note: Perform this activity with an adult. Wear safety goggles and use caution when handling hot objects.

Safety

Perform this activity with an adult. Wear safety goggles and use caution when handling hot objects.

ASSESS
Lesson Assessment: Crystal Shapes (*Offline*)

You will complete an offline assessment covering the main objectives of this lesson. Your learning coach will score this assessment.

Name _____   Date _____

Crystal Shapes

Rocks are made of two or more crystals. Each kind of crystal has its own special shape. The pattern of a crystal's shape is called a *lattice*. You've studied two kinds of lattices: cubic and hexagonal.

Fill in the name of the shape that stacks to create the pattern.

A cubic lattice is formed from stacked _____.

A hexagonal lattice is formed from stacked _____.

Procedure

1. Study the patterns. Color the faces of the patterns. The face is the part that will be on the outside after you fold the pattern.
2. Cut each pattern.
3. Fold each pattern on the lines.
4. Tape the tabs of each pattern together.

Observations

1. Check both shapes. Are all the faces showing on both crystals? _____

   _____

   _____

2. Study the following rocks from your kit: Rock 7, Rock 10, and Rock 14. Which appear to have a cubic lattice pattern? Which appear to have a hexagonal lattice pattern? _____

   _____

   _____

   _____

Investigation Idea

Ice has a hexagonal crystal structure. Observe ice for this pattern.

Crystal Shapes

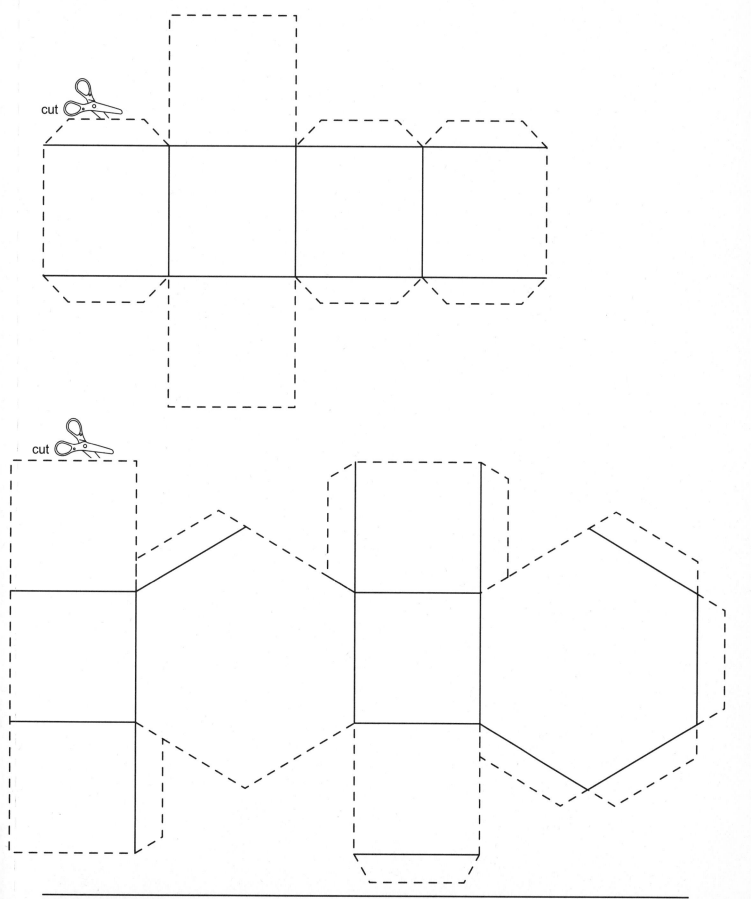

cut

cut

Name _____   Date _____

"Cool" Crystals

If one crystal cools quickly and another cools slowly, will that have an effect on the size of the crystals? Crystals are formed deep within the Earth so it is necessary to use a model to investigate this question. Use salt crystals to find out the answer to this question.

Hypothesis:
Will quick cooling result in larger or smaller crystals? Write a hypothesis to answer this question. Do not use the words *I think*. _____

_____

LAB SAFETY: Perform this activity with an adult. Wear safety goggles and use caution when handling hot objects.

Materials
goggles
heat source
pot
oven mitts
water – 300 mL
Epsom salts - 600 mL
spoon
two baby food jars (or plastic cups)
pipe cleaners
magnifying lens
ruler

Procedure
1. Wrap two pipe cleaners around a pencil so that one end hangs down about 1 cm above the bottom of the jar.
2. Heat the water until it is near boiling.
3. Stir in Epsom salts until they are dissolved.
4. Fill the baby food jars half way with the solution.
5. Lay the pencil with the pipe cleaners on top of the jar so the pipe cleaner hangs down.

"Cool" Crystals

1. Place one jar in the refrigerator to cool and the other in a place in the room where it will not be disturbed.
2. Observe the crystals at the times listed in the chart. After 4 hours, use the ruler to measure the crystal sizes.
3. Record all data in the chart.

Scientist Notebook
Circle what you change in the experiment (independent variable).
Underline what will happen because of the change (dependent variable).

Rate of cooling   Size of crystals   Amount of salt

Amount of water   Height of pipe cleaner   Color of pipe cleaner

Observations
Write your cup observations in the spaces on the chart. Record the size of the largest crystals after 4 days in the Measurement column.

Cup	Day 1	Day 2	Day 3	Day 4	Measurement
A					
B					

"Cool" Crystals

Analyze

1. In which jar did crystals form the fastest? The slowest? _____

_____

_____

2. In which jar did the smallest crystals form? The largest? _____

_____

_____

Conclusion

1. The crystals were cooled the fastest in the refrigerated jar. The crystals in the other jar cooled the slowest. What is the effect of how fast the crystals were cooled on their size? _____

_____

_____

2. Check the hypothesis you made. Did you prove it?_____

_____

_____

Investigation Idea

Repeat the experiment in this investigation with sugar, table salt, and rock salt. Compare their crystal shapes and sizes.

Name _____ Date _____

Lesson Assessment

Circle the letter of the word that completes the sentence.

1. The special shapes in crystals show a pattern called a _____.
   a. hexagon
   b. cube
   c. lattice
   d. mineral

2. Label the crystal shapes with the name of their type of pattern.

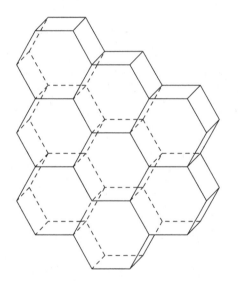 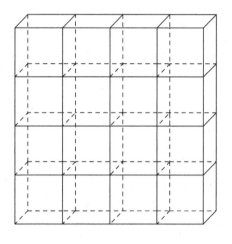

_____   _____

3. Some crystals are formed quickly when volcanic rock cools. How would those crystals compare to rock crystals that are formed over hundreds of years, deep in the Earth? Why? _____

   _____

   _____

   _____

Student Guide
Lesson 3: Properties of Minerals

The rocks that we see around us are built up of different kinds of minerals. Identifying minerals and learning about their properties are the first steps toward understanding rocks.

Lesson Objectives

- Recognize that you can identify minerals by their color, luster, hardness, streak, and specific gravity.

PREPARE

Approximate lesson time is 60 minutes.

Advance Preparation

- In this science lesson, your student will be using the rock kit. For the first few lessons in this unit, we don't want her to know the identity of the different rocks and minerals. Remove the lid with the key from the box, and set it aside for later reference.
- A white, porcelain streak plate is included in K12's additional science materials. If you do not have the plate, you will need to purchase at a home improvement store. The plate is a 2 inch piece of white ceramic tile.

Materials

For the Student

    📖 Mystery Information List

    📖 Mystery Minerals

    coin - penny

    household item - porcelain streak plate

    flashlight

    K12 Rocks and Minerals Kit

    nail, iron

    📖 Mineral Information List

    📖 Specific Gravity

    bowl - 2 liter

    spring scale

    string - 60 cm

    water

Keywords and Pronunciation

dolomite (DOH-luh-miyt)

galena (guh-LEE-nuh)

Hematite (HEE-muh-tiyt)

luster : The way light reflects off the surface of a mineral, or its shine. A silver coin has a metallic luster.

mica (MIY-kuh)

olivine (AH-luh-veen)

pyrite (PIY-riyt)

spinel (spuh-NEL)

LEARN

Activity 1: Qualities of Minerals *(Online)*

Activity 2: Be a Geologist *(Offline)*

Practice your skills as a geologist as you test mystery minerals and identify them based on their color, luster, hardness, and streak. See how many you can get correct--you may be headed for a career on the rocks!

Safety

As usual, you may wish to preview any books or websites listed in this lesson.

Activity 3. Optional: Specific Gravity *(Offline)*

If you think you are ready for the big time in geology, put your minerals through a specific gravity test.

ASSESS

Lesson Assessment: Properties of Minerals (*Online*)

Have an adult review your answers to the Mystery Minerals activity and input the results online.

Name _____   Date _____

Mineral Information List

Mineral	Color	Luster	Streak	Hardness	Specific Gravity
Fluorite	White, blue, green, red, yellow, purple	Glassy	Colorless	4	3-3.2
Feldspar	Gray, white, pink	Glassy	Colorless	6	2.5
Topaz	White, pink, yellow, pale blue	Glassy	Colorless	8	3.5
Pyrite	Gold	Metallic	Black	6	5.2
Quartz	Colorless, milky	Glassy	Colorless	7	2.6
Talc	Grayish, white	Dull	White	1	2.8
Gypsum	Colorless, white	Glassy	White	2	2.3
Hornblende	Dark green	Glassy	Pale gray	5.5	3.2
Calcite	Colorless, white	Glassy	Colorless, white	3	2.7
Halite	Colorless, light pink or red	Gassy	White	2 - 2.5	2.2

Name _____   Date _____

Mystery Minerals

Imagine a conversation like this:

FRIEND: I found this big hard lump in my backyard--I think I found gold!
YOU: Are you sure you've found real gold?
FRIEND: It's gold colored. Of course it's gold! Right?

What would you say to your friend?

Geologists test minerals in many different ways before saying for sure what substances are in them. Those tests include color, as your friend observed. But they also include hardness, luster, streak, and specific gravity. Each mineral has its own properties that make it different from all other minerals.

Test the items in your kit and find out what minerals they contain.

Materials

Nail	K12 Rocks & Minerals Kit
Penny	Flashlight
Streak plate	Magnifying Glass

Remove minerals 10, 11, 12, 13, 14, and 15 from your K12 Rocks and Minerals Kit. Perform each of the following tests on each mineral, and record your observations in the table provided.

Test 1: Color
Use the magnifying glass to observe each sample. Describe the color of each sample and write your observations in the chart on page 2.

Test 2: Luster
Hold each sample up to the sunlight or under the flashlight. Observe and record how light reflects off it. Luster may be a metallic shine, a glassy radiance, or a pearly shimmer.

Test 3: Streak
Use each mineral to draw a line across the streak plate. Observe and record the color of each streak.

Mystery Minerals

Test 4: Hardness

Use your fingernail, the copper penny, and the nail to test the hardness of each mineral. Try to scratch each sample with these items. Try to scratch each sample with each of the other minerals. Give each sample a number from Moh's Scale of Hardness that describes its hardness. A number 1 on the scale is the softest, while 10 is the hardest.

Observations

Mineral	10	11	12	13	14	15
Color						
Luster						
Streak						
Hardness						
Mineral name						

Analysis

Use your observations and study the Mineral Information List to figure out the identity of each mineral. Write their names in the last column in the chart.

Conclusion

1. How are the minerals you tested different from each other? _____

   _____

2. When scientists study things, they organize them into groups, or *classify* them, based on what they have in common. How does classifying make science easier? _____

   _____

3. Check your answers for mineral names. Did you have any that were incorrect? What do scientists do when testing to make sure they get their tests right? _____

   _____

Name _____   Date _____

Specific Gravity

Density can be used to identify any substance. Minerals have definite chemicals inside them, as well as physical characteristics on the outside. Density can be used to identify minerals based on these characteristics.

Sometimes, two minerals are too close in density to be identified. In that case, scientists measure the minerals' specific gravities. *Specific gravity* is simply a comparison of the mass of a mineral to the volume of water it displaces. Try this investigation to find the specific gravities of rocks from your K12 Rocks & Minerals Kit. Then compare your results to the specific gravities listed in the Mineral Information List.

Materials

2- liter bowl   water
string, 60 cm   feldspar
hornblende   quartz
hematite   talc
gypsum   calcite
pyrite   spring scale

Procedure
1. Fill the bowl about three-fourths with water.
2. Tie string around the mineral and make a loop in the other end.
3. Hook the string to the spring scale and measure the mass of the mineral in grams. Write the mass on the chart in the column "Mass Out of Water"
4. Keeping the mineral hanging on the scale, lower it into the water in the bowl. Do not allow the mineral to rest on the bottom or sides of the bowl. Write the mass on the chart in the column "Mass in Water."
5. Subtract the mineral's Mass in Water from its Mass Out of Water. Write this new number in the "Mass Displaced" column.
6. Divide the mineral's Mass Out of Water by its Mass Displaced. (Mass Out of Water ÷ Mass Displaced.) This is your mineral's specific gravity. Compare your findings to the Mineral Information List.

Specific Gravity

Mineral	mass out of water (g)	mass in water (g)	mass displaced (g)	specific gravity (g)
Feldspar				
Hornblende				
Quartz				
Hematite				
Talc				
Gypsum				
Calcite				
Pyrite				

Name _____ Date _____

Lesson Assessment

Properties of Minerals

For the questions below, review your student's responses on the Mystery Mineral activity and input the results online.

1. Follow the procedures in the attached Mystery Minerals activity and, using the information gathered during the experiments and recorded in the Observations table, identify the following minerals:

   Mineral 10: _____

   Mineral 11: _____

   Mineral 12: _____

   Mineral 13: _____

   Mineral 14: _____

   Mineral 15: _____

Student Guide
Lesson 4: Mining of Minerals

There are over 90 minerals that humans use in different industries. These minerals are found inside the Earth and must be mined. Once mined, people must take these minerals from rocks and process them. In this lesson you will learn about some activities involved in getting the minerals we use.

Lesson Objectives
- Define ore as rock with a high metal content.
- Describe the activity of producing aluminum from bauxite as an example of processing ore.
- Describe some of the everyday uses of minerals.

PREPARE

Approximate lesson time is 60 minutes.

Materials
For the Student
- Minerals All Around
- Minerals Around the World Map
  household item - see Minerals All Around sheet
  pencil

Keywords and Pronunciation
ore : Rock with a high metal content. Bingham Canyon Mine processes a great deal of copper ore.
surface mining : A form of mining that strips off the surface layer of earth and digs down to the mineral-containing layers. Huge explosions at the surface-mining site lifted layers off of the ground for the miners.
talus (TAY-luhs)

LEARN
Activity 1: Metals from the Earth (Online)

Activity 2: If It Can't be Grown, It Has to Be Mined (Offline)
Forks, spoons, dishwashers and microwave ovens--what do they all have in common? They are made from minerals. But minerals can be found in every room of the house, not just the kitchen. Learn more about how things you use every day are made from minerals.

ASSESS

Lesson Assessment: Mining of Minerals (*Offline*)

You will complete an offline assessment covering the main objectives of this lesson. Your learning coach will score this assessment.

LEARN

Activity 3: Visit the Mineral Information Institute (*Online*)

There is a lot to learn about minerals and mining. Did you know that the mineral *gold* has played an important role throughout history? Visit the Mineral Information Institute to learn about gold and many other minerals. Go to the next screen to get started.

Safety

As usual, you may wish to preview any books or websites listed in this lesson.

Name _____   Date _____

Minerals All Around

Almost all of the things we use every day are made from minerals. All the items you use at home, at play, to do work, and even some things we eat come from minerals that are mined from the Earth.

Look around your house for the following objects. Observe the objects and predict what minerals might be in them. Then, look them up on the chart called Minerals All Around. Were you surprised?

Minerals can be found in countries all around the world. Some countries, such as the U.S. and Russia, have many different minerals mined from them. Where do all of the minerals come from that make up the paper this is written on, or the pencil you are using? Use the Where in the World chart to record the countries where the minerals can be found.

Common household items	Minerals I predict may be in them	Minerals actually in them	Where they are mined
drinking glass			
fruit juice			
pencil			
soda can			

How could a friend who doesn't know much about minerals see where they come from? A map! You now have all the information you need to show where in the world these minerals come from. Think of a symbol, such as a triangle or star, for each mineral in your table. Use these symbols to show what countries they are mined in on the world map. Be sure to create a key so that your friend can read your map.

Name _____ Date _____

Minerals All Around

Baby Powder: Talc
Batteries: Antimony, Cadmium, Lead, Zinc
Bicycle: Aluminum, Clay, Diatomite, Mica Sulfur, Selenium, Wollastonite, Zinc
Books: Clay, Limestone, Sodium Sulfate, Feldspar
Bricks: Bauxite, Chromite, Zircon, Silica, Graphite, Kyanite, Andalusite, Sillimanite, Clays
Cake/Bread: Gypsum, Phosphates
Car: Platinum, Iron, Aluminum, Lead, Coal, Barite, Boron, Calcium Carbonate, Bentonite, Silica, Chromium, Perlite, Wollastonite, Mica, Industrial Diamonds, Zeolite, Clays
Carpet: Calcium Carbonate, Limestone
Clothing: Boron, Halite, Molybdenum, Sulfur
Desk: Copper, Iron, Zinc, Nickel
Digital Alarm Clock: Boron, Copper, Gold, Quartz
Drinking Glass: Boron, Silica
Drinking Water: Limestone, Lime, Salt, Fluorite
Fruit Juice: Perlite, Diatomite
Glass/Ceramics: Silica sand, Limestone, Talc, Lithium, Borates, Soda Ash, Feldspar
Ink: Calcium Carbonate
Lights: Aluminum, Copper, Beryllium (fluorescent), Tungsten (incandescent), Tin, Nickel
Linoleum: Calcium Carbonate, Clay, Wollastonite
Kitty Litter: Attapulgite, Montmorillonite, Zeolites, Diatomite, Pumice, Volcanic Ash

Paint: Titanium Oxide, Clays, Limestone, Mica, Talc, Silica, Copper, Fluorspar, Iron, Tungsten, Zinc, Cadmium
Paper: Boron, Clay, Kaolin, Sulfur, Talc, Titanium, Trona
Pencils: Graphite, Clay
Pencil Sharpener: Iron, Copper, Zinc
Plastic: Limestone, Wollastonite, Coal, Talc, Silica, Petroleum Products
Pots and Pans: Aluminum, Iron, copper
Potting Soil: Titanium Dioxide, Kaolin Clays, Calcium Carbonate, Mica, Talc, Silica, Wollastonite
Skateboard: Aluminum, Calcium Carbonate, Clay, Coal, Iron, Mica, Sulfur, Silica, Talc, Wollastonite
Soda Can: Aluminum
Sports Equipment: Graphite, Fiberglass
Telephone: Aluminum, Beryllium, Coal, Copper, Gold, Iron, Limestone, Silica, Silver, Talc, Wollastonite
Television set: Aluminum, Antimony, Barite, Beryllium, Cobalt, Columbium, Copper, Europium, Gallium, Germanium, Gold, Indium, Iron, Kaolin, Lanthanides, Limestone, Lithium, Manganese, Mercury, Mica, Molybdenum, Platinum, Rhenium, Selenium, Silica, Strontium, Tantalum, Tellurium, Terbium, Tin, Titanium, Vanadium, Yttrium, Zinc, Zirconium
Toothpaste: Calcium Carbonate, Limestone, Sodium Carbonate, Fluorite
Wallpaper: Mica, Trona

Name _____   Date _____

Minerals All Around: Where in the World

Aluminum (Bauxite)............................	Australia, Guinea
Andalusite..	South Africa, India
Barite..	China, India
Beryllium..	U.S., Russia
Borates..	Turkey, U.S.
Cadmium..	Japan, Belgium
Chromite..	South Africa, Russia
Clays...	U.S.
Copper...	Chile, U.S.
Diatomite...	U.S., France, Romania
Feldspar...	Italy, U.S.
Fluorspar...	China, Mongolia
Graphite...	Korea, India
Gravel..	U.S.
Gypsum..	U.S., Canada
Industrial Diamonds...........................	Australia, Zaire
Iron...	Russia, China
Kyanite..	SouthAfrica, India, France
Lead..	Australia, U.S.
Lime..	Russia, China
Limestone...	U.S.
Micas...	U.S., Russia
Nickel..	Russia, Canada
Perlite..	U.S., Greece
Platinum...	South Africa, Russia
Potash..	Russia, Canada
Pumice...	Italy, Greece
Selenium..	Japan, Canada
Silica Sand.......................................	U.S., Netherlands
Sillimanite..	South Africa
Sodium Sulfate..................................	Mexico, Spain
Sulfur..	U.S., Russia
Talc...	Japan, U.S.
Tin..	China, Brazil
Titanium...	Russia, Japan
Trona (Soda Ash)...............................	U.S., Kenya
Tungsten..	China, Russia
Vermiculite.......................................	South Africa, U.S.
Wollastonite......................................	Germany, Great Britain
Zeolites..	U.S., Tanzania
Zinc...	Canada, Australia
Zircon..	Australia, South Africa

Name _____

Date _____

Minerals Around the World

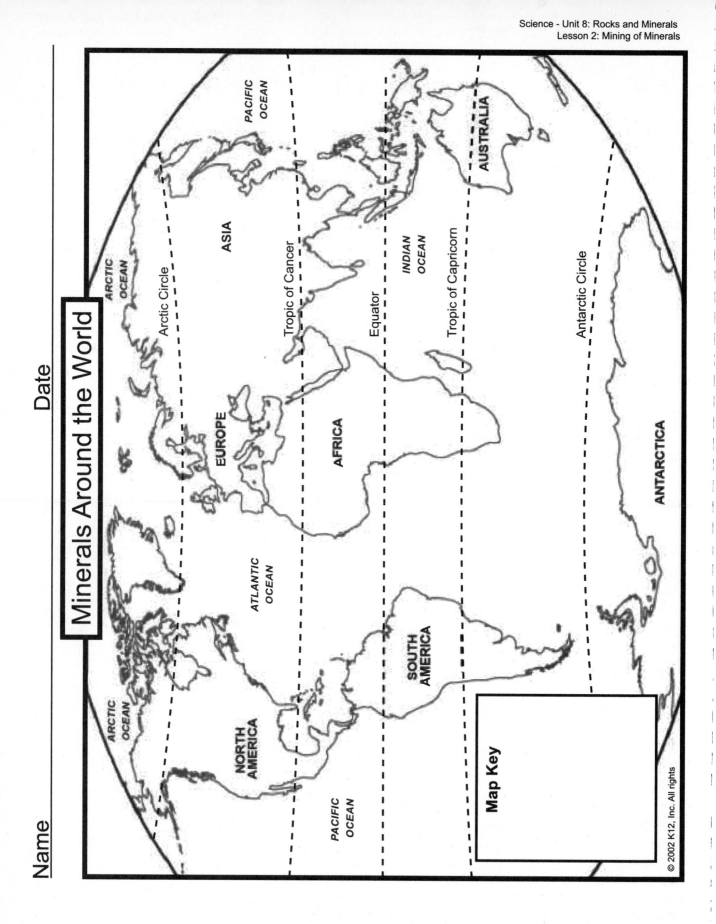

PACIFIC OCEAN

ARCTIC OCEAN

ASIA

AUSTRALIA

Arctic Circle

Tropic of Cancer

Equator

INDIAN OCEAN

Tropic of Capricorn

Antarctic Circle

EUROPE

AFRICA

ANTARCTICA

ATLANTIC OCEAN

NORTH AMERICA

SOUTH AMERICA

ARCTIC OCEAN

PACIFIC OCEAN

Map Key

Name _____   Date _____

Mining of Minerals Assessment

1. Rock that contains minerals and has a high metal content is called

   _____.

2. We use minerals in our everyday lives. Name one mineral you use

   every day. _____

   Tell what the mineral is used in. _____

   _____

   _____

   _____

3. Bauxite is an ore that contains many minerals including aluminum.
   Put the steps involved in processing bauxite in order by writing the
   numbers 1-4 in the blanks below.

   _____ The melted aluminum metal is poured into molds to cool.

   _____ Machines at a refinery crush the ore, clean it, and heat it
          to produce a pure chemical high in the element aluminum.

   _____ Open-pit mining removes bauxite from the ground.

   _____ A hot furnace called a *smelter* purifies the aluminum.

Name _____   Date _____

Minerals All Around

Almost all of the things we use every day are made from minerals. All the items you use at home, at play, to do work, and even some things we eat come from minerals that are mined from the Earth.

Look around your house for the following objects. Observe the objects and predict what minerals might be in them. Then, look them up on the chart called Minerals All Around. Were you surprised?

Minerals can be found in countries all around the world. Some countries, such as the U.S. and Russia, have many different minerals mined from them. Where do all of the minerals come from that make up the paper this is written on, or the pencil you are using? Use the Where in the World chart to record the countries where the minerals can be found.

Common household items	Minerals I predict may be in them	Minerals actually in them	Where they are mined
drinking glass			
fruit juice			
pencil			
soda can			

How could a friend who doesn't know much about minerals see where they come from? A map! You now have all the information you need to show where in the world these minerals come from. Think of a symbol, such as a triangle or star, for each mineral in your table. Use these symbols to show what countries they are mined in on the world map. Be sure to create a key so that your friend can read your map.

Name _____ Date _____

Minerals All Around

Baby Powder: Talc
Batteries: Antimony, Cadmium, Lead, Zinc
Bicycle: Aluminum, Clay, Diatomite, Mica Sulfur, Selenium, Wollastonite, Zinc
Books: Clay, Limestone, Sodium Sulfate, Feldspar
Bricks: Bauxite, Chromite, Zircon, Silica, Graphite, Kyanite, Andalusite, Sillimanite, Clays
Cake/Bread: Gypsum, Phosphates
Car: Platinum, Iron, Aluminum, Lead, Coal, Barite, Boron, Calcium Carbonate, Bentonite, Silica, Chromium, Perlite, Wollastonite, Mica, Industrial Diamonds, Zeolite, Clays
Carpet: Calcium Carbonate, Limestone
Clothing: Boron, Halite, Molybdenum, Sulfur
Desk: Copper, Iron, Zinc, Nickel
Digital Alarm Clock: Boron, Copper, Gold, Quartz
Drinking Glass: Boron, Silica
Drinking Water: Limestone, Lime, Salt, Fluorite
Fruit Juice: Perlite, Diatomite
Glass/Ceramics: Silica sand, Limestone, Talc, Lithium, Borates, Soda Ash, Feldspar
Ink: Calcium Carbonate
Lights: Aluminum, Copper, Beryllium (fluorescent), Tungsten (incandescent), Tin, Nickel
Linoleum: Calcium Carbonate, Clay, Wollastonite
Kitty Litter: Attapulgite, Montmorillonite, Zeolites, Diatomite, Pumice, Volcanic Ash

Paint: Titanium Oxide, Clays, Limestone, Mica, Talc, Silica, Copper, Fluorspar, Iron, Tungsten, Zinc, Cadmium
Paper: Boron, Clay, Kaolin, Sulfur, Talc, Titanium, Trona
Pencils: Graphite, Clay
Pencil Sharpener: Iron, Copper, Zinc
Plastic: Limestone, Wollastonite, Coal, Talc, Silica, Petroleum Products
Pots and Pans: Aluminum, Iron, copper
Potting Soil: Titanium Dioxide, Kaolin Clays, Calcium Carbonate, Mica, Talc, Silica, Wollastonite
Skateboard: Aluminum, Calcium Carbonate, Clay, Coal, Iron, Mica, Sulfur, Silica, Talc, Wollastonite
Soda Can: Aluminum
Sports Equipment: Graphite, Fiberglass
Telephone: Aluminum, Beryllium, Coal, Copper, Gold, Iron, Limestone, Silica, Silver, Talc, Wollastonite
Television set: Aluminum, Antimony, Barite, Beryllium, Cobalt, Columbium, Copper, Europium, Gallium, Germanium, Gold, Indium, Iron, Kaolin, Lanthanides, Limestone, Lithium, Manganese, Mercury, Mica, Molybdenum, Platinum, Rhenium, Selenium, Silica, Strontium, Tantalum, Tellurium, Terbium, Tin, Titanium, Vanadium, Yttrium, Zinc, Zirconium
Toothpaste: Calcium Carbonate, Limestone, Sodium Carbonate, Fluorite
Wallpaper: Mica, Trona

Name _____   Date _____

Minerals All Around: Where in the World

Aluminum (Bauxite).................	Australia, Guinea
Andalusite..........................	South Africa, India
Barite...............................	China, India
Beryllium...........................	U.S., Russia
Borates.............................	Turkey, U.S.
Cadmium............................	Japan, Belgium
Chromite...........................	South Africa, Russia
Clays...............................	U.S.
Copper.............................	Chile, U.S.
Diatomite..........................	U.S., France, Romania
Feldspar...........................	Italy, U.S.
Fluorspar..........................	China, Mongolia
Graphite...........................	Korea, India
Gravel..............................	U.S.
Gypsum.............................	U.S., Canada
Industrial Diamonds...............	Australia, Zaire
Iron................................	Russia, China
Kyanite............................	SouthAfrica, India, France
Lead................................	Australia, U.S.
Lime................................	Russia, China
Limestone..........................	U.S.
Micas...............................	U.S., Russia
Nickel..............................	Russia, Canada
Perlite.............................	U.S., Greece
Platinum...........................	South Africa, Russia
Potash.............................	Russia, Canada
Pumice.............................	Italy, Greece
Selenium...........................	Japan, Canada
Silica Sand........................	U.S., Netherlands
Sillimanite........................	South Africa
Sodium Sulfate.....................	Mexico, Spain
Sulfur..............................	U.S., Russia
Talc................................	Japan, U.S.
Tin.................................	China, Brazil
Titanium...........................	Russia, Japan
Trona (Soda Ash)...................	U.S., Kenya
Tungsten...........................	China, Russia
Vermiculite........................	South Africa, U.S.
Wollastonite.......................	Germany, Great Britain
Zeolites............................	U.S., Tanzania
Zinc................................	Canada, Australia
Zircon..............................	Australia, South Africa

Student Guide
Lesson 5: The Rock Cycle

Few things seem more changeless than rocks. So you would think that of all the things in nature, rocks are some of the most stable. Over long periods of time, however, rocks change. In fact, they can change in many ways, recycling their minerals into the same or other kinds of rocks. This fascinating process is called *the rock cycle*.

Lesson Objectives

- Identify the three different types of rocks and how they form.
- Describe what is meant by the term *rock cycle*.

PREPARE

Approximate lesson time is 60 minutes.

Materials

For the Student

🖳 Rock Formation

K12 Rocks and Minerals Kit

🖳 Rock Recipes

pencil

butter - 75 g (2 1/2 tbls.)

chocolate chips - 75 g (1/2 cup)

egg

flour - 150 g (1 cup + 2 tbls.)

household item - vanilla (1/2 tsp.)

measuring spoon

sugar - 125 g (2/3 cup)

bowl - large mixing

cookie sheet - greased

measuring cup

spoon

Keywords and Pronunciation

gneiss (niys)

igneous (IG-nee-uhs) : A class of rocks that forms from magma and lava. Obsidian may look like black glass but, in fact, it is a kind of igneous rock.

metamorphic (meh-tuh-MOR-fik) : A class of rocks that forms when heat and pressure act on igneous or sedimentary rock.

metamorphosis (meh-tuh-MOR-fuh-suhs) : the process of change in the shape or composition of rocks, caused by heat, pressure, or chemical reactions acting over time

rock cycle : The pathways by which rocks change from one form to another over time. Igneous rocks and metamorphic rocks are part of the rock cycle.

sediment : Layers of rock and mud that form at the bottom of lakes, streams, rivers, and oceans. The sediment at the bottom of the bay is mostly mud.

sedimentary : Rocks that form when other rocks layer and fuse with each other. Sandstone is a kind of sedimentary rock.

LEARN
Activity 1: Ever-Changing Rocks *(Online)*
Safety
As usual, you may wish to preview any books or websites listed in this lesson.

Activity 2: Rock Formation *(Offline)*
What do sandstone, gneiss, and obsidian have in common? They are all examples of one of the main types of rock--sedimentary, metamorphic, and igneous. Take a closer look at these rocks and review where they form.

Activity 3: Rock Recipes *(Online)*
Have you ever helped cook a meal in which you had to follow a recipe? What were the ingredients like? In this activity you will be asked to write some recipes of your own, but they are not for things you can eat--they are recipes for rocks!

ASSESS
Lesson Assessment: The Rock Cycle (*Offline*)
You will complete an offline assessment covering the main objectives of this lesson. Your learning coach will score this assessment.

LEARN
Activity 4. Optional: Metamorphic Rock Cookies *(Offline)*
What do chocolate chip cookies and metamorphic rocks have in common? The ingredients for chocolate chip cookies are something like the minerals in metamorphic rock. When you heat the mixture, it changes it into something else--in this case, a yummy treat!

Activity Instructions:
125 g (2/3 cup) sugar
1 egg
75 g (1/2 cup) chocolate chips
150 g (1 cup + 2 Tbls) flour
75 g (2 ½ Tbls) butter, softened
½ teaspoon vanilla

---

1. Preheat the oven to 375 degrees.
2. Cream the butter and sugar together until the mixture is light and fluffy.
3. Beat in the egg and add the vanilla.
4. Slowly add the flour.
5. Stir in the chocolate chips.
6. Drop spoonfuls of cookie dough onto a greased cookie sheet, leaving 3 cm between each cookie.
7. Bake the cookies for 10-15 minutes or until they are golden brown. While they cool, explain how the chocolate chip cookies are like metamorphic rocks. When they are cool, enjoy your metamorphic treat!

Safety

This lesson involves eating or working with food. Before beginning, check with your doctor, if necessary, to find out whether your student will have any allergic reaction to the food.

Name _____   Date _____

Rock Formation

Many of the samples in your rock kit are examples of sedimentary, metamorphic or igneous rock. Take the pumice, basalt, limestone, sandstone, marble and gneiss samples out of the kit.

Match each item on the left to its correct description on the right.

igneous rock O

pumice O

basalt O

metamorphic rock O

marble O

gneiss O

sedimentary rock O

limestone O

sandstone O

O A class of rocks formed when heat and pressure act on igneous or sedimentary rock. Marble, which is an example of this kind of rock, forms under great pressure.

O This metamorphic rock is dark but looks like it has stripes of minerals running through it. The visible crystals make it shimmer.

O This rock is formed by cooled lava filed with gas bubbles. It is white or light gray and might look like a rock froth.

O Layers may be visible in this reddish-brown sedimentary rock.

O Rocks that form when other rocks are cemented together. Sandstone is an example of this kind of rock.

O This metamorphic rock is white and sparkles with crystals that are easy to see.

O A class of rocks formed from magma and lava.

O This rock is volcanic rock, so it is igneous. It is dark gray and very hard. You may see holes in it made by gas bubbles.

O This whitish-gray sedimentary rock is powdery, with few visible crystals.

Rock Formation

Study the picture below. Use the words from the Word Bank to correctly label the picture.

Word Bank

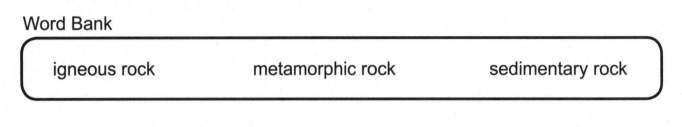

igneous rock   metamorphic rock   sedimentary rock

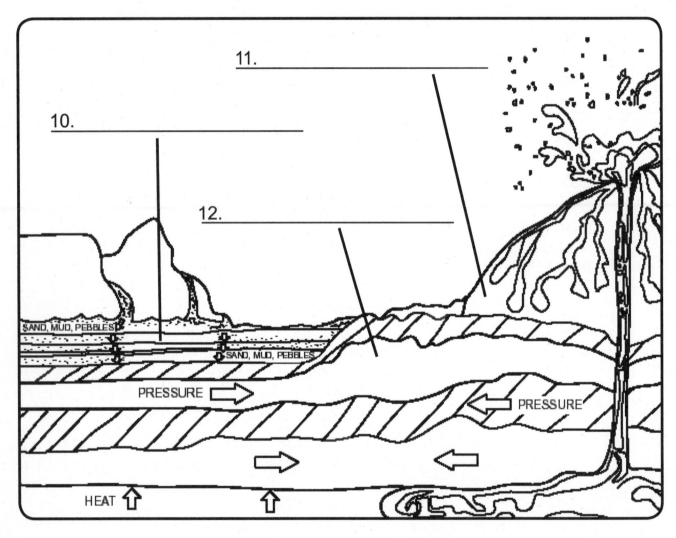

Name _____   Date _____

Rock Recipes

You have learned how it takes several different factors to make up sedimentary, metamorphic, and igneous rocks, such as minerals, heat, and pressure. You can think of each of these components as an ingredient that goes into the "recipe" for each rock. Look at the example recipe card for igneous rocks, and then write your own recipe for metamorphic and sedimentary rocks.

Title <u>Igneous Rock Recipe</u> _____

Ingredients <u>1 part metamorphic or sedimentary rock</u>
_____ <u>25 parts heat</u> _____

_____

Directions <u>Heat the rocks to 1,400°C for 6 hours to form</u>
<u>magma. Allow the magma to cool to form an igneous rock.</u>

_____

_____

Rock Recipes

Title _____

Ingredients _____

_____

_____

Directions _____

_____

_____

_____

Title _____

Ingredients _____

_____

_____

Directions _____

_____

_____

_____

Name _____   Date _____

The Rock Cycle Assessment

1. Which of the following best describes the rock cycle?
   A. The rock cycle is a process in which pressure causes sediment particles to cement together.
   B. The rock cycle is a series of processes in which one kind of rock is transformed into other kinds.
   C. The rock cycle is a series of processes in which water, wind, or waves break up rocks.
   D. The rock cycle is a process in which heated magma cools to form igneous rock.

2. Write the word *metamorphic, sedimentary,* or *igneous* in front of the statement that best describes how each is formed.

   _____ These rocks form when bits of rock are compacted by pressure and cement together to form new rocks.

   _____ These rocks form when other rocks are subjected to large amounts of pressure, heat, or chemical reactions.

   _____ These rocks form in volcanoes and wherever magma pushes through the Earth's crust.

The Rock Cycle Assessment

3. Label the different parts of the rock cycle where igneous, sedimentary, and metamorphic rock are formed.

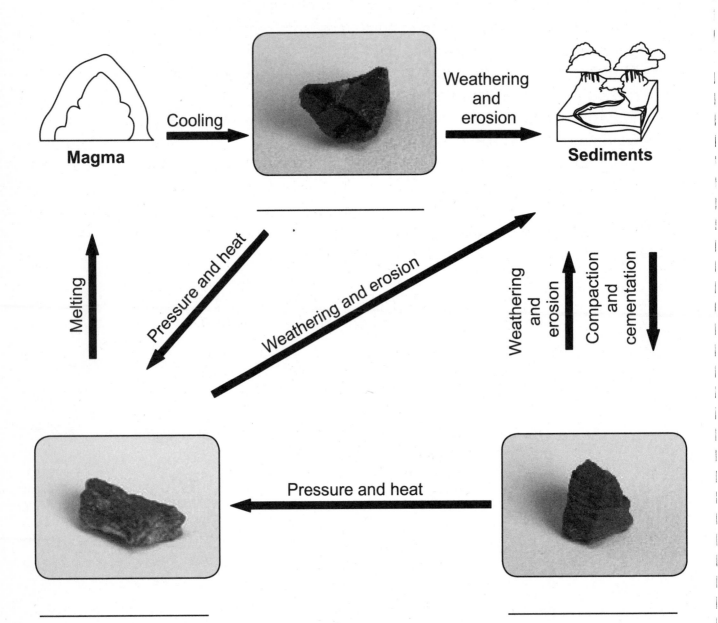

Student Guide
Lesson 6: Drifting Continents

The great movements of the earth happen both on and below its surface. Magma from the mantle is constantly moving, exerting a powerful force on the crust above. Huge plates on the surface rearrange themselves like moving puzzle pieces. Take a look at how this *continental drift* has occurred throughout the earth's long history.

Lesson Objectives

- Describe Alfred Wegener's theory of continental drift.
- Explain that earth's crust is made up of rigid plates that are always moving.
- Describe three types of plate boundaries.

PREPARE

Approximate lesson time is 60 minutes.

Materials

For the Student
- 🖥 Pangaea Puzzle
- paper, construction, 9" x 12"
- scissors
- 🖥 Plate Boundaries
- pencil
- 🖥 Mountain Models
- clay
- hairpins
- household item - roll of calculator paper
- tissue paper - two or three colors
- cardboard - sheet 12 x 20 inches
- ruler, metric
- tape, masking

Keywords and Pronunciation

Alfred Wegener (AHL-frayt VAY-guh-nuhr)

Himalaya (hih-muh-LAY-uh)

oceanic (oh-shee-A-nihk)

Pangaea (pan-JEE-uh) : the name scientists give to a supercontinent that once existed on earth

San Andreas (san an-DRAY-uhs)

Theory of Plate Tectonics : the scientific theory that earth's crust is made up of about 20 huge plates that are always moving very slowly

LEARN
Activity 1: Pangaea Puzzle *(Offline)*

Can you name the seven continents? Scientists think that long ago, all seven continents were a part of one huge continent, which they name *Pangaea*. Before you learn more about why scientists think the continents have drifted apart, put together your Pangaea Puzzle.

Activity 2: Movement of Continents *(Online)*

Activity 3: Plate Boundaries *(Offline)*

Amazing things can happen when the edges of plates move. Review what happens when plates push against each other or slide past each other.

ASSESS

Lesson Assessment: Drifting Continents (*Online*)

You will complete an offline assessment covering the main objectives of this lesson. Your learning coach will score this assessment.

LEARN
Activity 4. Optional: Mountain Models *(Offline)*

Have you ever seen a mountain form itself? Of course not—it takes a long, long time. Complete the activity on the Mountain Model sheet to see what happens when two continental plates collide with each other.

Name _____   Date _____

Pangaea Puzzle

Cut out the pieces from the world map and place them on a piece of construction paper. Move the pieces around to see how they might have fit together to form Pangaea. You will see how they come together in the Explore section.

Name_____   Date_____

Plate Boundaries

Look at the pictures of the different plates moving against each other. Describe what is happening in each picture and what the results may be.

Description:_____

_____

_____

_____

Results:_____

_____

_____

_____

Description:_____

_____

_____

_____

Results:_____

_____

_____

_____

Description:_____

_____

_____

_____

Results:_____

_____

_____

_____

Name _____ Date _____

Lesson Assessment

Drifting Continents

1. Alfred Wegener developed a theory of continental drift that ultimately was adopted by most scientists. What is the continental drift theory?

   _____

   _____

   _____

2. The continents continue to drift, mountains form, volcanoes erupt, and earthquakes occur. These all happen because the Earth's crust is made up of rigid _____ that are always moving.

   A. slides

   B. rocks

   C. plates

   D. trays

3. Describe what happens when an oceanic and a continental plate push against each other.

   _____

   _____

   _____

4. Describe what happens when two continental plates push against each other.

   _____

   _____

   _____

5. Describe what happens when two plates slide against each other in opposite directions.

   _____

   _____

   _____

Name _____ Date _____

Mountain Model

Complete the following steps to make your Mountain Model. Use the illustration to help you.

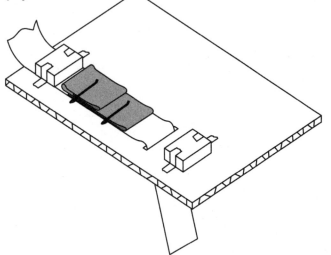

1. In a 50 cm by 30 cm piece of cardboard, cut a slit that is 10 cm long.
2. Cut a piece of calculator paper so that it is at least 75 cm long.
3. Form pieces of clay into two blocks that are the same width of the paper and about 5 cm high. These will represent the two plates.
4. Thread one end of the calculator paper through the slit so that you can pull it from the bottom of the cardboard.
5. Use masking tape to secure one of the clay blocks at the end of the cardboard about 1 cm behind the slit. Tape the other block on the end of the paper that is on top of the cardboard.
6. Cut tissue paper into strips as wide as the paper. Use hairpins to attach four layers of tissue paper directly in front of the clay block at the end of the paper.
7. Slowly pull on the paper coming out of the bottom of the cardboard so that the clay block at the end moves toward the slit.
8. Continue to pull on the paper until it can't move any more and observe what happens.

What happened to the tissue paper when the two blocks collided? _____

_____

_____

Student Guide
Lesson 7: Volcanoes

Volcanoes are among the most awesome things on the Earth's surface. Often they explode with tremendous force. They can cause great destruction, as well as fiery displays of light and noise. Find out what volcanoes are and what causes them, and learn about the different types.

Lesson Objectives

- Identify the main parts of a volcano: magma chamber, vent, and crater.
- Identify and describe the three types of land volcanoes (cinder cone, composite, and shield).
- Explain how volcanoes are formed.

PREPARE

Approximate lesson time is 60 minutes.

Materials

> For the Student
>
> > 🖥 Volcanoes
> >
> > pencil

Keywords and Pronunciation

lava : magma that is extruded to the surface of the Earth´s crust

magma : Molten rock that is under the surface of the earth. The upper crust and lower mantle are places where magma is found.

Paricutin (pahr-REE-koo-teen)

volcano : Any areas of the Earth in which magma is extruded to the surface. Most volcanoes are situated at the edges of continental plates.

LEARN
Activity 1: The Fire from Below *(Online)*
Safety
As usual, you may wish to preview any books or websites listed in this lesson.

Activity 2: Volcanoes *(Offline)*
You have learned a lot about the different types of volcanoes. Review these volcanoes and the parts that make up each of them.

ASSESS

Lesson Assessment: Volcanoes (*Online*)

You will complete an online assessment covering the main objectives of this lesson. Your assessment will be scored by the computer.

LEARN

Activity 3. Optional: Volcanoes Around the World (*Offline*)

Visit Volcano World to discover volcanoes in countries all around the world.

Name _____   Date _____

Volcanoes

You have learned about three types of land volcanoes: cinder cone, shield and composite. Label each of these volcanoes. Then, on the lines below each volcano, write a description of each and how it formed. If needed, look back at the Explore section to help you.

_____   _____   _____
_____   _____   _____
_____   _____   _____
_____   _____   _____
_____   _____   _____
_____   _____   _____
_____   _____   _____

Label the magma chamber, vent and crater on the picture of the volcano below.

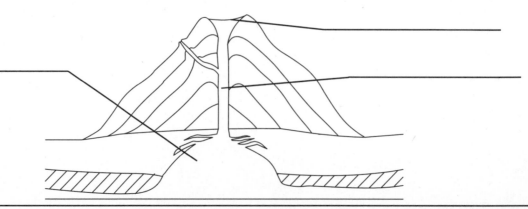

Student Guide
Lesson 8: Earthquakes

Lots of things change in life, but you'd think the Earth under your feet wouldn't be one of them. One experience with an earthquake, though, can change your *mind*--and fast. Earthquakes are fascinating and frightening events of nature. Why do they happen? Can we predict when they will strike? How is the Earth itself changed after a massive quake?

Lesson Objectives

- State that an *earthquake* is the shaking or sliding of the Earth's surface.
- Explain how a *seismograph* is used to determine earthquake activity.
- Describe how the *Richter scale* is used to measure an earthquake's magnitude.

PREPARE

Approximate lesson time is 60 minutes.

Materials

For the Student

🖳 Model Seismograph

cardboard box - 30 cm (12 in) each side

hole punch - (single punch)

household item - Paper cup, 5 oz. (2)

marbles

marker, black water soluble

paper, adding machine tape

pencil

ruler, metric

scissors

string

tape, masking

🖳 Earthquake!

household item - glue

household item - paper

thumbtacks

wood block - 2 of same size

Keywords and Pronunciation

epicenter : The point on the Earth's surface that is right above the focus of an earthquake. The greatest damage was done at the epicenter of the quake.

fault : A break in the Earth's crust along which plates move. The San Andreas Fault in California is the site of many earthquakes.

focus : The point where the movement of the plates started. The earthquake that caused so much damage had a focus deep within the Earth.

Richter (RIHK-tuhr)

seismograph (SIYZ-muh-graf) : An instrument used to record earthquake waves. The seismograph recorded a large earthquake at 10:05 a.m.

seismologist (siyz-MAH-luh-jist)

tsunami (tsou-NAH-mee)

LEARN
Activity 1: The Big Shake *(Online)*
Safety
As usual, you may wish to preview any books or websites listed in this lesson.

Activity 2: Model Seismograph *(Offline)*
Scientists use seismographs to measure earthquake activity. The lines drawn on the paper help the scientists determine the magnitude of the earthquake on the Richter scale. Make your own seismograph, and then brace yourself for the quakes!

ASSESS
Lesson Assessment: Earthquakes (*Online*)
You will complete an online assessment covering the main objectives of this lesson. Your assessment will be scored by the computer.

LEARN
Activity 3. Optional: Earthquake! *(Offline)*
Make a model of an earthquake using two wooden blocks, a piece of paper, and some thumbtacks. Watch what happens when the "earth" shakes during the great quake.

Safety
Caution your student to be careful when working with the thumbtacks in the Beyond the Lesson activity.

Name _____ Date _____

Model Seismograph

Follow the steps below to make your own seismograph.

1. Turn the box on its side so that the opening is facing you. Cut the flaps off of each side of the box so that the opening is not blocked.

2. Cut a circle with a 4 cm (2 in.) diameter in the center of the top of the box.

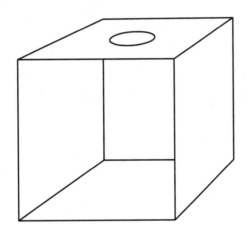

3. Cut two slits in the box. The slits should be 1 cm x 8 cm (1/2 in x 4 in.). The first slit should be made in the center of the bottom of the box, close to the edge. The second slit should be lined up with the first one, but made at the back of the box.

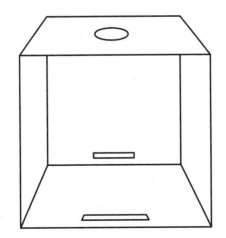

Model Seismograph

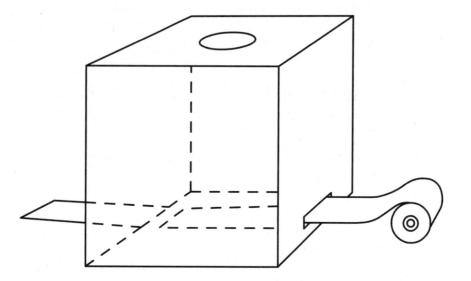

4. Place the roll of adding tape at the back of the box so that the end of the paper comes over the top of the roll. Thread the paper through the slit at the back of the box and then down into the slit at the front.

5. Use a hole punch to make two holes below the rim of the cup, one on each side. Then use a pencil to poke a hole in the center of the bottom of the cup.

6. Thread a 60 cm (24 in.) piece of string through the two holes in the sides of the cup.

7. Lay a pencil across the hole in the top of the box and tape the two ends of the string to it.

8. Push the tip of a marker through the bottom of the cup. Add some small rocks or marbles to the cup to act as weights.

9. Turn the pencil at the top of the box until the tip of the pen barely touches the paper beneath it, then tape the string to secure it at this length to the pencil. Tape the ends of the pencil to the top of the box.

Model Seismograph

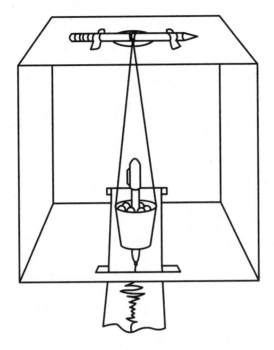

10. Pull the end of the paper forward with one hand as you gently shake the box with your other hand. The shaking will simulate an earthquake.

11. Repeat step 10 to simulate a second earthquake, this time shaking the box a little bit harder.

The pen in the cup made markings on the paper as you pulled it. What happened to the markings as you shook the box to simulate an earthquake? _____

_____

How can you tell by looking at the paper which earthquake was stronger? _____

_____

What is the name of the scale that scientists use to determine the magnitude of an earthquake?_____

_____

_____

Name _____ Date _____

Earthquake!

You have learned that earthquakes occur when two continental plates slide against each other moving in opposite directions. Build a model of an earthquake to explore what happens as the ground shakes.

Directions

1. Place the two wooden blocks side-by-side lengthwise. Glue a piece of paper on top of the blocks. Be careful not to get glue in between the blocks or they will not slide against each other.
2. Carefully lay some thumbtacks on top of the paper with the pointed sides up.
3. Push the ends of the blocks in opposite directions. Observe what happens.

Questions

1. What do the two wooden blocks represent? _____

_____

2. What happened when you pushed the two blocks in opposite directions? _____

_____

_____

3. How does this activity show what happens during an earthquake?

_____

_____

_____

_____

Student Guide
Lesson 9: Rocks and Minerals Unit Review and Assessment

The United States Geological Survey (USGS), is a government agency that collects, monitors, and analyzes information about natural resources in the United States and around the world. They have an information center people can call to ask questions about rocks, minerals, volcanoes, earthquakes--anything about the Earth.

Today, you have been asked to volunteer at the information center and answer some calls. Don't worry--if you need help, you can ask your boss, Paula.

Lesson Objectives

- Explain that rock is composed of different combinations of minerals.
- Recognize that you can identify minerals by their color, luster, hardness, streak, and specific gravity.
- Identify and describe the properties of the Earth's layers: crust, mantle, outer core, and inner core.
- Recognize that minerals have their own distinct crystal shape, determined by the arrangement of their atoms.
- Differentiate among igneous, sedimentary, and metamorphic rocks by referring to their properties and methods of formation.
- Explain that the surface of the Earth is made up of rigid plates that are in constant motion, and that the motion of these plates against, over, and under each other causes earthquakes, volcanoes, and the formation of mountains.
- Identify the various structures of volcanoes, describe the types of eruptions that form them, and explain how they change the landscape.
- Describe what happens during an earthquake and how the landscape can change as a result.
- Recognize that ore is rock with a high metal content, and that most metals come from minerals mined from the Earth's crust.
- Explain how a *seismograph* is used to determine earthquake activity.
- Describe how the *Richter scale* is used to measure an earthquake's magnitude.

PREPARE

Approximate lesson time is 60 minutes.

LEARN
Activity 1: On Call! *(Online)*

ASSESS

Unit Assessment: Rocks and Minerals (*Offline*)

Complete an offline Unit Assessment. Your learning coach will score this part of the Assessment.

Name _____ Date _____

Rocks and Minerals Unit Assessment

1. In the space below, draw a picture of the Earth and label the four main layers. Then describe the properties of each layer on the lines below.

crust _____

_____

_____

mantle _____

_____

_____

outer core _____

_____

_____

inner core _____

_____

_____

Rocks and Minerals Unit Assessment

2. How are rocks different from minerals? _____

_____

_____

_____

The Earth is made up of rigid plates that are always moving. As these plates move, they can cause earthquakes to occur and mountains and volcanoes to form. In the spaces below, describe how the moving plates cause each to happen.

3. mountains _____

_____

_____

_____

_____

_____

4. volcanoes _____

_____

_____

_____

_____

_____

5. earthquakes _____

_____

_____

_____

_____

_____

Rocks and Minerals Unit Assessment

6. Earthquakes occur in different places around the world, especially in the areas within the Ring of Fire. Explain what happens to the Earth's surface during an earthquake, and how an earthquake can change the landscape around it._____

_____

_____

_____

_____

_____

Write *true* in front of each true statement. Write *false* in front of each false statement.

7. _____All minerals have the same type of crystal structure because all of their atoms are arranged the same way.

8. _____Ore is a mineral that contains a large amount of metal. Most minerals come from rock that is mined from the Earth's crust.

9. _____Scientists identify minerals by their color, luster, hardness, streak, and specific gravity.

Write the word from the Word Bank next to the statement that matches it.

Word Bank

cinder cone	Richter scale	vent	sedimentary
composite	volcano	ore	metamorphic
magma chamber	crater	igneous	shield
seismograph	earthquake		

Rocks and Minerals Unit Assessment

10. _____ The central collecting place for magma at the base of the volcano.

11. _____ This towering volcano forms from both lava flows and cinder rocks.

12. _____ A tool scientists use to measure earthquake activity.

13. _____ Rock with a high metal content.

14. _____ These rocks form when bits of rock are compacted by pressure and cement together to form new rocks.

15. _____ This is the top of the volcano where sulfur-filled gasses and lava come out.

16. _____ This type of volcano forms as lava spreads over a long distance and cools to form a hill with gentle slopes.

17. _____ These rocks form when other rocks are subjected to large amounts of pressure, heat, or chemical reactions.

18. _____ Scientists use this to measure the magnitude of an earthquake.

19. _____ These rocks form in volcanoes and wherever magma pushes through the crust.

20. _____ When lava comes up out of the ground for a long period of time, this type of volcano is formed.

21. _____ This stony tube runs up the center of the volcano. It may have many branches though which lava flows during an eruption.

Student Guide
Lesson 1: Weathering

Rocks and minerals are formed and broken down in the turbulent processes of Earth. Rocks formed in huge eruptions of lava may slowly fade away under forces of weathering--wind, water, and even the workings of living things. These bits of rocks and minerals may form huge sediments. So the Earth, which seems so unchanging is, in fact, always changing.

You have learned that the rock cycle is a continuous process that changes the forms of rocks over time. One of the main steps in the rock cycle is *weathering*, the breakdown of rocks. Learn how rocks get broken apart by nature's forces.

Lesson Objectives

- Identify examples of physical and chemical weathering.
- Describe different causes of weathering, such as ice, growth from plants, and acid rain.

PREPARE

Approximate lesson time is 60 minutes.

Materials

For the Student

    📖 Physical and Chemical Weathering

    clay

    cup, plastic (3)

    freezing source

    vinegar

    chalk

    markers

    plastic wrap

    spoon (2)

    water

Keywords and Pronunciation

deposition : The dumping of soil or rock particles in a place far from their origins. The glacier caused the deposition of a huge amount of weathered rock at the mouth of the river.

erosion : The movement of soil and broken rocks by wind, water, or other means. During the Dust Bowl era, wind caused great erosion of the soil.

lichen (*LIY-kuhn*)

mass wasting : The movement down a slope of a body of rock and/or soil due directly to gravity. Mass wasting can be rapid, as when a landslide or mudflow occurs, or it can be slower, as in a slow creep of a hillside downhill.

sediment : The layers of rock or soil that result from their transport and deposition. The sediment at the bottom of the lake originated as soil on the nearby hills.

---

weathering : the breakdown of rocks by physical or chemical processes; weathering causes the rocks on a cliff to wear away

LEARN
Activity 1: The Breakdown of Rocks *(Online)*

Activity 2: Physical and Chemical Weathering *(Offline)*
In this activity you will experiment with physical and chemical weathering. These processes break down rocks on the surface of the Earth. Both contribute to the ultimate erosion of rocks.

ASSESS
Lesson Assessment: Weathering (*Online*)
You will complete an online assessment covering the main objectives of this lesson. Your assessment will be scored by the computer.

Name _____   Date _____

Physical and Chemical Weathering

Activity 1

1. Moisten two clumps of clay and roll them into two balls.
2. Wrap each ball with plastic wrap. Place one ball in the freezer, and leave one out on the counter for 24 hours.
3. After 24 hours, unwrap the two balls and compare them.

Do the two clay balls still look the same? If not, explain how they look different. _____

_____

_____

_____

Is this an example of chemical or physical weathering? _____

_____

_____

_____

Activity 2

1. Break the piece of chalk into three pieces. Place one piece in each of the three cups.
2. Using a marker, write the word *water* on the first cup and *vinegar* on the second.
3. Observe what happens as you pour enough water into the first cup to cover the chalk. Record your answer in the table below. Do the same to the piece in the second cup, this time using vinegar.
4. Place the remaining piece of chalk in the third cup.
5. Set the experiment aside for a couple of days, or until the vinegar and water have evaporated. Compare the chalk in the first two cups to the chalk in the third cup. Record your observations in the table on the next page.

Physical and Chemical Weathering

	Immediately after adding the liquid	After the liquid has evaporated
Chalk in water		
Chalk in vinegar		

Is what happened to the chalk an example of chemical or physical weathering? _____

_____

_____

_____

What in nature is causing weathering like the vinegar? _____

_____

_____

_____

Student Guide
Lesson 2: Soils

You have been studying a lot about minerals and rocks lately. There is another element to geology as well-- soil. You might think of it as just the dirt beneath your feet. But soil is the very stuff of our lives. Soils are what plants grow in, and plants are the beginning of any food chain. Soils differ widely from place to place and have a lot to them. They are a far cry from "just dirt."

Lesson Objectives

- Describe a soil profile and explain how different horizons are formed.
- Describe properties of various soil types.

PREPARE

Approximate lesson time is 60 minutes.

Advance Preparation

- For this science lesson, you will need three 2-liter plastic bottles.

Materials

For the Student

   📖 What's in Your Soil?

   bottle, plastic - (2 liter) (3)

   household item - craft stick

   household item - newspaper

   household item - shovel

   soil - samples

   magnifying glass

   markers - permanent

   plastic wrap

   ruler, metric

   scissors

Keywords and Pronunciation

fertile : Capable of supporting plant growth. The gardener said that the lush growth of petunias was due to the fertile soil.

horizon : One of the layers in a soil profile. The A horizon of my soil sample was loaded with earthworms and ants.

humus (HYOO-muhs) : Organic matter in the soil, which is the remains of decayed and decaying living things. The farmer was happy with the new land because the soil was rich in humus.

LEARN
Activity 1: Amazing Soil *(Online)*

Activity 2: What's in Your Soil? *(Offline)*
There are many different types of soil containing rocks, particles and organic matter. Explore some soil samples from where you live to see what they are made up of.

Safety
Be careful where you help your student dig up the soil. Check with your local utility company to find out where electrical lines may be buried.

ASSESS
Lesson Assessment: Soils (*Offline*)
You will complete an offline assessment covering the main objectives of this lesson. Your learning coach will score this assessment.

Name _____   Date _____

What's In Your Soil?

You have learned that soil is a mixture of weathered rock, humus, air, and water. Soils from different areas can be made up of different amounts of these materials. Compare three different soil samples to see what they are made of. Go to different areas to collect them. As you gather your samples, you should be digging down deep enough to be able to observe some horizon layers.

1. Cut the tops off of three 2-liter plastic bottles. These will be used to hold your soil samples.
2. Gather your samples by going to three different locations. Using your shovel, outline a circle and try to dig straight down. For each sample, dig about 20 cm (8 in.) below the surface. Push the top of the empty bottle down through the dirt, carefully lifting it out with the sample inside.
3. Use a permanent marker to label the bottles, noting where each sample was taken from.
4. Look at each sample through the bottle to see if you can clearly observe different layers in the soil. Think about what you have learned about the horizons in a soil profile. Record which horizon(s) your sample contains in the Soil Chart on the next page.
5. Spread three sheets of newspaper out on a large, flat surface. Gently take each sample out of the bottles and place them onto separate pieces of newspaper. Be careful not to mix the samples.
6. Use a magnifying glass to study the contents of each sample. A craft stick can be used to spread the soil around so that things can be seen more clearly. Look for any animals, rocks, plants or decaying material. What type of parent soil do you think this is? Remember, sandy soils have large mineral particles. Clay has small particles. Silts have medium-sized particles. Record your observations in the chart on the next page.
7. Carefully fold the sides of the newspaper up, and pour each sample back into its bottle.
8. Add enough water to each bottle so that it stands at least 4 cm above the soil. Use a different spoon to stir up each sample for about a minute. Allow the samples to sit for a day. Sketch the sample and then describe it in the columns on the next page.

Name _____

Date _____

What's In Your Soil?

	Location	Soil horizons	Contents	Watered sample sketch	Watered sample description
Sample 1					
Sample 2					
Sample 3					

Name _____   Date _____

Soil Assessment

Jim and Laura need your help. They have always dreamed of owning their own farm where they can grow their own crops. They want to start looking for a piece of property to start their farm on, but they heard that they need to make sure the soil is good for planting. Jim and Laura know that there are different types of soil, but they don't know much about each of them. Answer Jim and Laura's questions below to help them out. Use the illustration to help you.

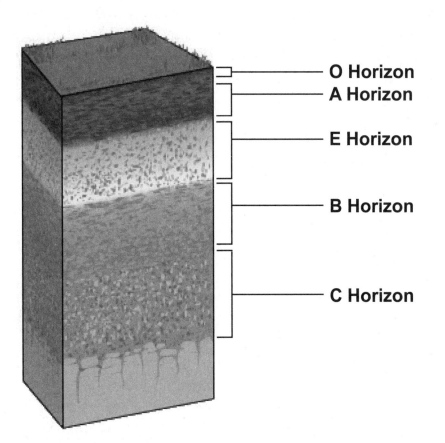

- O Horizon
- A Horizon
- E Horizon
- B Horizon
- C Horizon

Jim wants to know what a soil profile is. Can you explain it to him? _____

_____

_____

_____

_____

_____

Soil Assessment

Laura knows that the top two layers of a soil profile are called *topsoil*. What are some of the things that can be found in the topsoil?

_____

_____

_____

_____

Both Jim and Laura don't know much about the different types of soil. Jim thinks that clay soil is the best kind to grow crops in, but Laura thinks that sand and silt are the best types of soil for plants. Explain the different types of soil for them. Be sure to let them know which type(s) of soil are best them to plant their crops in.

Clay:_____

_____

_____

_____

Silt:_____

_____

_____

_____

Sand:_____

_____

_____

_____

Student Guide
Lesson 3: Erosion and Deposition: Gravity and Water

Soil forms from broken rocks and minerals, humus, air, and water. Soil, too, is a part of the great recycling of materials on Earth. It can be uprooted from its place of origin and moved away by the forces of gravity and water. Erosion and mass wasting remove soil and other materials from the land.

Lesson Objectives
- Describe how the slope of the land affects erosion.
- Describe how gravity and moving water weather, erode, and shape the surface of the land by transporting sediment from one location to another, where it is deposited.

PREPARE

Approximate lesson time is 60 minutes.

Materials
For the Student

    🖳 Water Erosion

    clay - modeling

    cup, plastic - 8 oz

    drinking glass

    drinking straw

    household item - 3 books

    soil

    cookie sheet

    measuring cup

    paper towels

    pencil

    water

Keywords and Pronunciation
deposition : The settling of rock and soil after it has been transported by forces causing erosion. The river was blocked by the deposition of soil after the mudslide.

erosion : The movement of soil and rock by agents such as gravity, water, glaciers, and wind. The Badlands of South Dakota show evidence of erosion by wind.

mass wasting : The movement down a slope of a body of rock and/or soil due directly to gravity. Mass wasting can be rapid, as when a landslide or mudflow occurs, or it can be slower, as in a slow creep of a hillside downhill.

tributary : A smaller river or creek that carries water into a larger river. The Ohio River is a tributary of the Mississippi River.

V-shaped valley : A valley shaped like a V in cross section, the shape of which is caused by water. Many valleys in California are V-shaped valleys, formed by rushing water.

LEARN
Activity 1: Powers of Gravity and Water *(Online)*

Activity 2: Water Erosion *(Offline)*
Does the slope of the land affect the amount of erosion by water? Complete this activity to see for yourself.

ASSESS
Lesson Assessment: Erosion and Deposition: Gravity and Water *(Online)*
You will complete an online assessment covering the main objectives of this lesson. Your assessment will be scored by the computer.

Name _____   Date _____

Water Erosion

The surface of the Earth is covered with different types of landforms, from small hills to huge, towering mountains. Even though they are different in height, rainfall and gravity working together can cause erosion in all of them.

In this activity, you will run a test to see how the slope of the land affects the amount of water erosion that can occur. A cookie sheet covered in soil will act as the land. A cup filled with water will act as the rainfall. You will run three trials in this experiment, first with one book under one end of the cookie sheet, then with two books, and then finally with three books. The books under the cookie sheet with create a slope in the land like that of a hill or mountain. After you make your prediction, take your supplies outside and perform the activity.

Prediction

Do you think that there will be more water erosion when the "land" is sloped with one, two, or three books? _____

_____

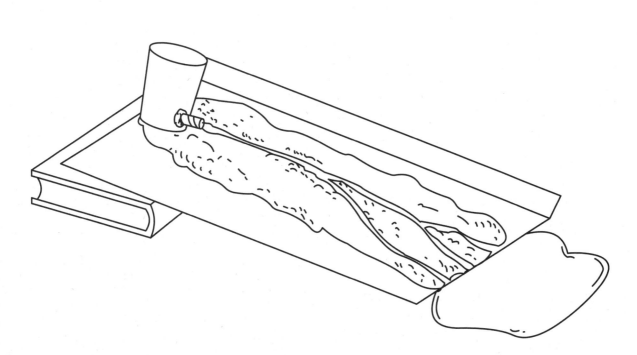

Water Erosion

Procedure
1. Fill a drinking glass with water and set it aside.
2. Use a pencil to make a hole in the side of a paper cup. The hole should be down near the bottom of the cup.
3. Cut a straw in half and insert one of the halves into the hole in the cup. Hold the straw in place by sealing it to the cup with bits of clay.
4. Lay a cookie sheet on a flat surface and use a measuring cup to cover it with a thin layer of soil. Place a book under one end of the cookie sheet.
5. Place the cup on the raised end of the cookie sheet.
6. Cover the hole of the straw with your finger as you fill the cup with water.
7. Remove your finger and observe what happens.
8. Use a paper towel to remove the soil and dry off the cookie sheet between each trial. Repeat steps 4-7 with two books and then three books under the cookie sheet. Be sure to use the same amount of soil each time.

What happened when you took your finger off the end of the straw and let the water come out? _____

_____

_____

What two things caused the erosion to happen in the experiment? _____

_____

_____

Did more erosion occur with one, two or three books under the cookie sheet? Was your prediction correct? _____

_____

How does this show whether or not slope affects the amount of erosion that occurs? _____

_____

_____

Student Guide
Lesson 4: Erosion, Transport, and Deposition: Glaciers and Wind

We have seen that gravity and water are two forces that cause the erosion of rocks and soil. Two others are glaciers and wind. Although glaciers may not seem to affect most of us, they have caused huge changes in the land where many live. Wind is more easily noticed. It is easy to see how wind can pick up soil particles and carry them far away.

Lesson Objectives

- Describe how glaciers are formed and differentiate between the continental and valley glaciers.
- Explain how glaciers move to erode and reshape the surface of the land.
- Describe how wind erodes and weathers the surface of the land.

PREPARE

Approximate lesson time is 60 minutes.

Advance Preparation

- You will need to prepare an ice block ahead of time for this science lesson. Place a cup of water with bits of sand, gravel, and clay into a plastic container and place in the freezer overnight.

Materials

For the Student

   🖥 Glaciers

      cardboard box - top, large with sides

      clay

      freezing source

      gravel

      household item - additional lamp

      household item - plastic container

      household item - plastic container top

      sand

      soil

      lamp

      ruler

      water

Keywords and Pronunciation

glacier (GLAY-shur) : A mass of ice that arises from years of snow adding up. The glacier ended at the ocean where huge chunks of ice fell into the sea.

moraine (muh-RAYN) : The mass of earth and ice pushed to the front or side of a moving glacier. Most of the high ports in northern Long Island in New York State are parts of an old moraine.

U-shaped valley : A valley that is rounded at the bottom; formed and given its characteristic shape by a glacier that once inhabited it. There are many U-shaped valleys in Alaska.

LEARN

Activity 1: The Power of Ice and Wind *(Online)*

Activity 2: Glacial Erosion *(Offline)*

As glaciers erode the land, they change it a great deal. In this activity, you will make a glacier of your own and see how this erosion occurs.

ASSESS

Lesson Assessment: Erosion, Transport, and Deposition: Glaciers and Wind, Online (*Online*)

You will complete an online assessment covering the main objectives of this lesson. Your assessment will be scored by the computer.

Name _____   Date _____

Glaciers

Glaciers are big blocks of ice that may contain bits of rock and
soil. For this activity, you will need to make an ice block and allow
it to freeze before you can begin. If you have not already done so,
fill a plastic container with one cup of water and add bits of sand,
clay, and gravel. Place the container in the freezer and allow it to
freeze overnight.

Procedure

1. Fill the top of a cardboard box with soil so that it is at least 8
   cm (6 in.) deep.
2. Use a ruler to make a V-shaped river valley down the middle
   of the soil. Measure the channel's width and depth and record
   them on the table below.
3. Draw a sketch of the river channel in the box below. Be sure to
   include the measurements.
4. Take your glacier (ice block) out of the freezer and place it at
   the upper end of the river channel.
5. Using your fingers, gently push the glacier along the river
   channel until it is in the center of the box top.
6. Place a lamp over the middle of the box top and turn it on.
   Allow the ice to melt. Observe what happens and record it in
   the table.
7. Measure the depth and width of the valley created by
   the glacier.
8. Draw a sketch of the glacier valley including the
   measurements. Label the moraines and kettle lakes that may
   have formed.

Glaciers

	Width	Depth	Observation
River Valley			
Glacier Valley			

River Valley Sketch	Glacier Valley Sketch

The river valley that you formed in the soil was V-shaped. Describe the shape of the valley that was carved out by the moving glacier. _____

_____

_____

How can you tell how far down the glacier traveled? _____

_____

_____

_____

Student Guide
Lesson 5: Unit Review and Assessment

Wow! You have learned a lot about how land can be changed by weathering, erosion, and deposition. Help solve a mystery as you review for your Unit Assessment.

In this lesson you'll meet Mrs. Fussbudget. She is unhappy about a piece of land that she inherited. She thinks that someone has changed it. She doesn't seem to know much about what shapes the land, and how long it takes. Can you help her solve the mystery?

Lesson Objectives

- Describe a soil profile and explain how different horizons are formed.
- Explain both the physical and the chemical weathering of rocks, and be able to classify examples of each.
- Explain that *soil* is a mixture of weathered rock, humus, air, and water.
- Describe how gravity, moving water, wind, and glaciers weather, erode, and shape the surface of the land by transporting sediment from one location to another, where it is deposited.

PREPARE

Approximate lesson time is 60 minutes.

LEARN
Activity 1: Weathering Mystery *(Online)*

ASSESS

Unit Assessment: Weather, Erosion, Deposition (*Offline*)

Complete an offline Unit Assessment. Your learning coach will score this part of the Assessment.

Name _____ Date _____

Weathering, Erosion, and Deposition Unit Assessment

Weathering, erosion, and deposition cause changes to the Earth's surface. Gravity, running water, glaciers, and wind all play a part in shaping the land. On the lines below, explain what each of them is and describe some of the changes they cause.

1. glaciers: _____

_____

_____

_____

_____

_____

2. running water: _____

_____

_____

_____

_____

_____

3. gravity: _____

_____

_____

_____

_____

_____

4. wind: _____

_____

_____

_____

_____

Weathering, Erosion, and Deposition Unit Assessment

Use the words in the Word Bank to complete the sentences below.

Word Bank

humus	sediment	profile
water	air	physical
rock	topsoil	chemical

5. Acid rain happens when carbon dioxide mixes with the water in the Earth's atmosphere. Acid rain is an example of _____ weathering.

6. Soil is a mixture of humus, weathered rock, water and _____.

7. If you dug a deep hole in the surface of the Earth, you would see many different layers. The layers make up the soil _____.

8. Gravity, moving water, wind, and glaciers weather, erode, and shape the surface of the land by transporting _____ from one location and depositing it in another.

9. When water seeps into the cracks of a rock and then freezes, the ice pushes against the rock, causing it to split apart. This is an example of _____ weathering.

10. The top two layers of a soil profile are called _____.

Weathering, Erosion, and Deposition Unit Assessment

Label each type of erosion below as either physical or chemical and then tell what caused the erosion.

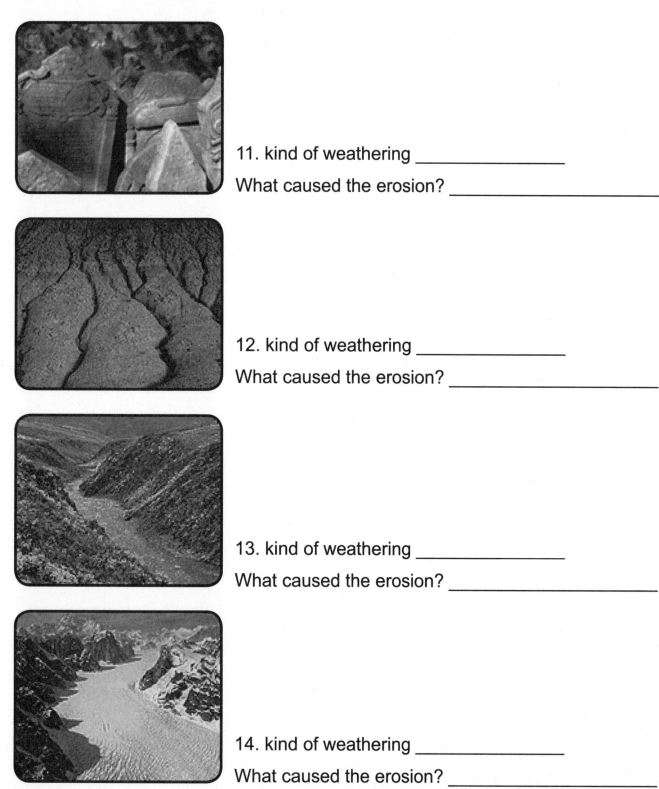

11. kind of weathering _____

What caused the erosion? _____

12. kind of weathering _____

What caused the erosion? _____

13. kind of weathering _____

What caused the erosion? _____

14. kind of weathering _____

What caused the erosion? _____

Student Guide
Lesson 1: Fossils and How They Form

Dinosaurs, trilobites, and many other once-living things left clues in fossils deep within layers of rock. Find out how fossils formed and meet some important paleontologists who use fossils as clues to the past.

How do we know what the organisms of the past looked like? Fossils are one clue that help scientists called *paleontologists* learn about the past. Come explore the world of fossils, and learn how fossils formed.

Lesson Objectives

- Explain that fossils provide information about organisms that lived long ago.
- State that a *fossil* is a trace, print, or remain of an organism preserved over time in a rock.
- Identify the conditions under which fossils may form.

PREPARE

Approximate lesson time is 60 minutes.

Advance Preparation

- You will need the book *The Fossil Record and the History of Life*, by Bridget Anderson, for all of the lessons in this unit. If you have not yet received this book, skip to the next unit and return to this one later.
- If you don't already have it, you will need dried black beans (1/2 cup), dried red beans (1/2 cup), and dried white beans (1/2 cup) for the Layering activity.

Materials

For the Student

Come Learn with Me: The Fossil Record and the History of Life by Bridget Anderson

📖 Layering

baking dish, rectangular - glass

food - 1/2 cup dried black beans

food - 1/2 cup dried red beans

food - 1/2 cup dried white beans

sand - 1 1/2 cups

bowl (3)

graduated cylinder

measuring cup

spoon

timer

Keywords and Pronunciation

dinosaur : Any animal belonging to a group of large reptiles that lived during the Mesozoic era. Triceratops was the largest horned dinosaur that walked the Earth.

fossil (FAH-suhl) : The trace, print, or remain of an organism preserved over time in rock. Fossils can tell us how dinosaurs looked as well as how they acted.

mammoth : A kind of ancient elephant with long, curving tusks and shaggy hair. Mammoths lived during the Ice Age.

mineral : A crystalline substance of regular atomic arrangement found in the earth. Rocks are made of two or more minerals.

paleontologist (pay-lee-ahn-TAH-luh-jist) : A scientist who studies prehistoric animal and plant life. The paleontologist examined the fossil for clues about the animal.

sedimentary rock : Rock formed from sediment (particles of sand, soil, and mud). Many fossils of dinosaurs were found deep within the sedimentary rock.

trilobite (TRIY-luh-biyt) : An extinct species of arthropod with three humps on each segment of its body. A trilobite fossil from the Paleozoic era found in the Burgess Shale gave paleontologists clues about the past.

LEARN

Activity 1: Let's Read! *(Online)*

Sometimes the most ordinary, familiar places have wonderful secrets. Sometimes they hold evidence of plants and animals that died out during Earth's ancient past. This evidence comes in the form of fossils.

Activity 2: Layering *(Offline)*

We can find fossils in many places--in rock formations, under ice, and even at the bottom of a lake. Experiment to discover how the layering of sediment at the bottoms of lakes creates fossils over time.

ASSESS

Lesson Assessment: Fossils and How They Form (*Online*)

You will complete an online assessment covering the main objectives of this lesson. Your assessment will be scored by the computer.

Name _____   Date _____

Layering

Follow the directions for the experiment, then answer the questions.

1. Pour 125mL (½ cup) of the white beans into a bowl.
2. Pour 125mL (½ cup) of the red beans into a second bowl.
3. Pour 125mL (½ cup) of the black beans into a third bowl.
4. Add ½ cup (125mL) of soil or sand to each bowl of beans.
5. Mix the beans and soil (or beans and sand) in each separate bowl.
6. Fill the baking dish halfway with water.
7. Slowly sprinkle the beans and soil (or beans and sand) mixture from one of the bowls into the water.
8. Wait 10 minutes and observe the layer.
9. Sprinkle the beans and soil (or beans and sand) mixture from another bowl into the water.
10. Wait 10 minutes and observe the layers now.
11. Add the last beans and soil (or beans and sand) mixture.
12. After 10 minutes, observe all three layers.

Draw the results after the final bowl of beans is added and 10 minutes have passed.

What happened to the soil or sand that was added with each bean layer? _____

Consider each layer of beans a new layer of earth. Which color beans represent the oldest layer of earth? _____
Why? _____

Which bean layer represents the youngest layer? _____
Why? _____

Student Guide
Lesson 2: Reading the Fossil Record

There are many types of fossils--petrified wood, cast, and mold fossils. Each fossil helps paleontologists unearth clues about the Earth's past and the organisms that lived during that time.

Lesson Objectives

- Explain that fossils help scientists reconstruct the history of life on Earth.
- State that fossils provide evidence that many kinds of organisms that once lived on Earth are now extinct.
- Identify the different types of fossils, such as petrified, cast, and mold.

PREPARE

Approximate lesson time is 60 minutes.

Advance Preparation

- If you don't already have it, you will need plaster of paris for the Make Your Own Fossil activity.

Materials

    For the Student

        Come Learn with Me: The Fossil Record and the History of Life by Bridget Anderson

        🖳 Make a Fossil

        clay

        household item - paper cup

        household item - petroleum jelly

        household item - rolling pin

        household item - wax paper

        plaster of paris

        seashell

        graduated cylinder

        spoon - plastic

        timer

Keywords and Pronunciation

amber : A hard, often yellowish substance formed from fossilized tree sap. The insect was fossilized in the hardened amber.

cast fossil : A fossil formed when minerals replace animal tissue. A cast fossil is a three-dimensional view of the fossil remains.

decompose : To rot or decay. A dead animal's body will decompose over time.

decomposition : The process by which organic materials decay. Decomposition helps break down dead plants and animals.

mineralization : The process by which minerals replace the tissues of a dead organism. During mineralization, the skeleton of a dead animal hardens into rock.

---

paleontologist (pay-lee-ahn-TAH-luh-jist) : A scientist who studies prehistoric animal and plant life. The paleontologist examined the fossil for clues about the animal.

sedimentary : Rock formed from sediment (particles of sand, soil, and mud). Sedimentary rock is an important part of the fossilization process.

sedimentary rock : Rock formed from sediment (particles of sand, soil, and mud). Fossils are often found in sedimentary rock throughout the world.

LEARN
Activity 1: Let's Read! *(Online)*

In many ways, scientists are like detectives. This is especially true of paleontologists. Learn how they use methods from many of the sciences
--chemistry, biology, geology--to investigate things that happened thousands of years ago.

Activity 2: Make Your Own Fossil *(Offline)*

Use some ordinary materials to create cast and mold fossils.

ASSESS

Lesson Assessment: Reading the Fossil Record (*Online*)

You will complete an online assessment covering the main objectives of this lesson. Your assessment will be scored by the computer.

LEARN
Activity 3. Optional: Paleontologists *(Online)*

Are there many scientists who choose to become paleontologists? Are there female paleontologists? Visit this site and find out!

Safety

As always, you may want to preview any recommended sites before your student views them.

Name _____ Date _____

Make a Fossil

Follow the directions to make a seashell cast, then answer the question below.

1. Using a rolling pin, roll a piece of clay onto a piece of wax paper. You may choose the color. The flattened piece of clay should be about 3cm high and 5cm wide.
2. Coat the seashell with petroleum jelly and press it into the clay. Carefully remove the seashell. Wipe the excess petroleum jelly from the clay.
3. Observe the imprint the shell made. You now have a mold of the seashell.
4. Use more clay to build a wall about 1cm high around the edge of the flattened piece of clay. Secure the clay wall to the flattened piece so there are no holes under the wall. You will need the wall to hold in the plaster of Paris, which is like a thick liquid.
5. Place 70mL of the plaster of Paris into the paper cup. Slowly add about 25mL of water while mixing with the plastic spoon. The mixture should be thick but able to be poured. Add more water if necessary.
6. Fill the seashell imprint to the top of the wall with the plaster mixture.
7. Wait about 30 minutes for the plaster to dry. It should be hard when you place your finger on it.
8. Remove the clay surrounding the cast. Now you have a cast of the seashell.

What information can paleontologists learn from fossils?

_____
_____
_____
_____
_____
_____

Student Guide
Lesson 3: The Ever-Changing Earth

The Earth is constantly changing. Earthquakes shift the surface of the Earth as the oceans of the world change the shoreline of every landmass. How have the plants and animals of the Earth survived these changes? Explore the scientific theories about the changing world through geologic time.

Lesson Objectives

- State that geologic time is divided into four sections: Precambrian, Paleozoic, Mesozoic, and Cenozoic.
- Recognize that scientists think that many kinds of organisms once lived on Earth have completely disappeared.
- Recognize that scientists think that some organisms alive today resemble organisms of the distant past.

PREPARE

Approximate lesson time is 60 minutes.

Materials

For the Student

Come Learn with Me: The Fossil Record and the History of Life by Bridget Anderson

📖 Solving the Riddles of Fossils

Keywords and Pronunciation

Cenozoic (see-nuh-ZOH-ihk)

continent : A great landmass on the surface of the Earth. The United States is located on the continent of North America.

Equus : The genus name scientists give to the group of animals that include modern horses. *Equus* is the only close relative of the Hyracotherium that lives today.

evolution : The gradual change of organisms over time. Through the process of evolution, species become well adapted to life on Earth.

extinct : No longer existing. If a type of organism is extinct, it has died out.

Hyracotherium : An early ancestor of the modern horse. *Hyracotherium* was a kind of small, dog-like animal that ate mostly fruits and plants.

Mesozoic (meh-zuh-ZOH-ihk)

Paleozoic (pay-lee-uh-ZOH-ihk)

Pangaea (pan-JEE-uh) : the name scientists give to a supercontinent that once existed on earth

Precambrian (pree-KAM-bree-uhn)

species (SPEE-sheez) : A group of organisms that share many characteristics and that can interbreed. Scientists think that species slowly changed throughout history as conditions changed on Earth.

LEARN

Activity 1: Let's Read (Online)

Our Earth has changed radically throughout history. Temperatures, scenery, and living creatures have changed a lot over time. The four main sections of what we call *geologic time* had very, very different living conditions. You may be surprised at what the evidence shows.

Activity 2: Solving the Riddles of Fossils (Offline)

Paleontologists solve riddles all the time. They find scraps of evidence--scraps that are sometimes very tiny-- and try to figure out what the evidence represents. Solve some fossil riddles yourself by reading clues and interpreting them.

ASSESS

Lesson Assessment: The Ever-Changing Earth (*Online*)

You will complete an online assessment covering the main objectives of this lesson. Your assessment will be scored by the computer.

Name _____ Date _____

Solving the Riddles of Fossils

Read each riddle, then solve it. (Hint: You'll find help in your text.)

1. I am a fossil of a fern that grew in the tropics. I was found in
    Antarctica, which is extremely cold. No one moved me, so why
    was I found in Antarctica?

    _____

2. I am a fossil of a coral that lived in the ocean. I was found on dry
    land, far from any ocean. If no one moved me, why would I be
    found in the middle of a continent?

    _____

    _____

3. I am a horse, but my ancestors didn't look anything like me. I'm
    much bigger than they are, and my teeth are a lot stronger. Why
    don't I look like earlier horses?

    _____

    _____

    _____

4. I am a fossil of an animal. A fossil of another animal was found in
    a younger layer of rock above me. He looks more like animals
    who are alive today than I do. Am I probably older or younger
    than the other fossil?

    _____

    _____

    _____

    _____

    _____

SUPER CHALLENGE: Name this era!
1. I am called the Age of Dinosaurs. _____
2. My name means *ancient life*, though sometimes I'm called the
    Age of Trilobites. _____
3. I am the era in which you live. _____
4. I am the longest period of geologic time. _____

Student Guide
Lesson 4: The Precambrian Time and Paleozoic Era

What was the Precambrian time and Paleozoic era like? What organisms lived then? What major events define the eras? Search into the past and uncover the worlds of the Precambrian time and Paleozoic era.

Lesson Objectives

- Name one major event that occurred during the Precambrian time.
- Name one major event that occurred during the Paleozoic era.
- Name one organism that lived on the Earth during the Precambrian time.
- Name one organism that lived on the Earth during the Paleozoic era.

PREPARE

Approximate lesson time is 60 minutes.

Materials

For the Student

Come Learn with Me: The Fossil Record and the History of Life by Bridget Anderson

What Did the Moon See?

Keywords and Pronunciation

amphibian (am-FIH-bee-uhn) : A vertebrate that spends part of its life in water and part of its life on land. Frogs, toads, and salamanders are amphibians.

brachiopod (BRAY-kee-uh-pahd)

cyanobacteria (siy-A-nuh-bak-TIHR-ee-uh) : Bacteria that were one of the first forms of life on Earth. The earliest known fossils are of cyanobacteria.

meteorite (MEE-tee-uh-riyt) : A rocky object in space that falls to Earth before it burns up. A meteorite that hit the Earth made a crater as large as a football field.

Paleozoic (pay-lee-uh-ZOH-ihk)

Pangaea (pan-JEE-uh) : the name scientists give to a supercontinent that once existed on earth

Precambrian (pree-KAM-bree-uhn)

sedimentary rock : Rock formed from sediment (particles of sand, soil, and mud). Fossils are often found in sedimentary rock throughout the world.

stromatolite : A large colony of cynabacteria that grows like a reef of coral. Colonies of cyanobacteria form stromatolites that look like stone pillars in the ocean.

stromatolites (stroh-MA-tl-iyts)

trilobite (TRIY-luh-biyt) : An extinct species of arthropod with three humps on each segment of its body. A trilobite fossil from the Paleozoic era found in the Burgess Shale gave paleontologists clues about the past.

LEARN

Activity 1: Let's Read! *(Online)*

Volcanoes, earthquakes, and crashing meteorites were all part of the Earth's early years. A long time passed before life came about. Lean about the Precambrian time and Paleozoic era in Earth's history.

Activity 2: Diary of the Past *(Offline)*

If you could have been a witness to Earth's earliest years, what would you have seen? What would be your most important memories?

ASSESS

Lesson Assessment: The Precambrian Time and Paleozoic Era (*Online*)

You will complete an online assessment covering the main objectives of this lesson. Your assessment will be scored by the computer.

Name _____   Date _____

What Did the Moon See?

Imagine that you are the moon, looking down on the Earth. What would you have observed during the first two eras? Write your memories in this diary. The first entry has been written for you. Use the word bank below as you fill in the rest of your diary.

WORD BANK

stromatolites	trilobites	plankton
armor	canyon	worms	ferns
Pangaea	climate changes	salty seas
extinction	brachiopod	mudflows	sponge

Beginning of time: It's too dark to see much. There are a lot of meteorites, though, and they bang pretty hard. That poor planet is getting a lot of craters. There doesn't seem to be any life yet, but I'm optimistic. At this point there isn't even any oxygen, but I've already seen a lot of changes. At least the Earth is solid now-- at first there was only a ball of gas.

Precambrian: _____

_____

_____

_____

_____

_____

_____

_____

_____

_____

What Did the Moon See?

Paleozoic Era: _____

_____

_____

_____

_____

_____

_____

_____

_____

_____

Student Guide
Lesson 5: The Mesozoic and Cenozoic Eras

What were the Mesozoic and Cenozoic eras like? What organisms lived then? What major events define the eras? Search into the past and uncover the worlds of the Mesozoic and Cenozoic eras.

Lesson Objectives

- Name one major event that occurred during the Mesozoic era.
- Name one major event that occurred during the Cenozoic era.
- Name one organism that lived on the Earth during the Mesozoic era.
- Name one major event that occurred in each of the four geologic sections: Precambrian, Paleozoic, Mesozoic, and Cenozoic.

PREPARE

Approximate lesson time is 60 minutes.

Materials

> For the Student
>> Come Learn with Me: The Fossil Record and the History of Life by Bridget Anderson
>> 🖳 When Did It Happen?

Keywords and Pronunciation

asphalt : A black, tar-like substance. Asphalt fills The La Brea tar pits. Animals throughout the Cenozoic era became trapped in the tar.

Cenozoic (see-nuh-ZOH-ihk)

dinosaur : Any animal belonging to a group of large reptiles that lived in the Mesozoic era. Scientists think modern birds are descendants of Mesozoic dinosaurs.

ichthyosaur : An extinct marine reptile that lived in the Mesozoic era. Icthyosaurus had a dolphin-shaped body and a narrow, tooth-filled 'beak."

ichthyosaurus (ik-thee-uh-SAWR-uhs)

La Brea (luh BRAY-uh)

Mesozoic (meh-zuh-ZOH-ihk)

mosasaur (MOH-zuh-sawr) : An extinct marine reptile that lived in the Mesozoic era. Mosasaur had a long head, a large jaw, a strong and flexible neck, and two strong pairs of paddles.

oviraptor (oh-vih-RAP-tur) : A small, bird-like dinosaur that moved quickly on its two long legs. Oviraptor had a long tail, a curved neck, powerful jaws, and a strong beak.

plesiosaur (PLEE-see-uh-sawr) : An extinct marine reptile that lived in the Mesozoic era. Mary Anning, a female fossil collector, found the first plesiosaur fossil.

protoceratops (proh-toh-SEHR-uh-tahps)

pterosaur (TEHR-uh-sawr)

velociraptor (vuh-LAH-suh-rap-tuhr) : An extinct marine reptile that lived in the Mesozoic era. The velociraptor was a particularly vicious dinosaur.

LEARN
Activity 1: Let's Read! *(Online)*

How did the Earth look when dinosaurs were alive? How did it look when there was only one continent? Read pages 36 to 45 to learn about the evidence scientists have found.

Activity 2: When Did It Happen? *(Offline)*

The Mesozoic and Cenozoic Eras were very different. Using your book, tell which events and which organisms belong to each period.

ASSESS

Lesson Assessment: The Mesozoic and Cenozoic Eras (*Online*)

You will complete an online assessment covering the main objectives of this lesson. Your assessment will be scored by the computer.

LEARN

Activity 3. Optional: Were There Dinosaurs in Your Backyard? *(Online)*

Do scientists think dinosaurs lived in your backyard? Visit this site and find out!

Name _____ Date _____

When Did It Happen?

Some of these events happened in the Mesozoic Era, while others happened in the Cenozoic Era. Write an M next to each description that fits the Mesozoic Era, and write a C next to each description that fits the Cenozoic Era.

1.   Humans use fire for cooking.   _____
2.   Pangaea breaks apart.   _____
3.   Land animals begin to have live
     babies instead of laying eggs.   _____
4.   Continents move toward their
     current locations.   _____
5.   Dinosaurs live and roam the Earth.   _____
6.   Animals get stuck in LaBrea Tar Pits.   _____
7.   Temperature drops worldwide.   _____
8.   Plesiosaurs and oviraptors live.   _____
9.   Ice forms at north and south poles.   _____
10. The first large forests and open
     woodlands develop.   _____
11. Early humans make tools.   _____
12. A mass extinction occurs.   _____

For each of these sets of events, scientific evidence suggests which happened first, second, and last. Put the events in order by writing 1, 2, or 3 in the spaces provided.

13. A. Dinosaurs come into being.   _____
     B. Birds come into being.   _____
     C. Animals similar to crocodiles
        learn to run on their hind legs.   _____

14. A. Humans settle down to live in
        communities.   _____
     B Organisms adapt to colder
        environments.   _____
     C. Sea levels drop, exposing more land.   _____

Student Guide
Lesson 6: Unit Review and Assessment

What have you learned about fossils and geologic time? Play a game and review what you have learned about the earliest parts of Earth's history!

Lesson Objectives

- State that fossils provide evidence that many kinds of organisms that once lived on Earth are now extinct.
- Name one major event that occurred in each of the four geologic sections: Precambrian, Paleozoic, Mesozoic, and Cenozoic.
- Describe the conditions under which fossils may form and distinguish among the different types, such as petrified, mold, and cast.
- Explain that fossils provide information about organisms that lived long ago and help scientists reconstruct the history of life on Earth.
- Recognize that scientists divide geologic time into four main sections (Precambrian, Paleozoic, Mesozoic, and Cenozoic) and that each section covers one major stage in Earth's history.

PREPARE

Approximate lesson time is 60 minutes.

Materials

For the Student

🖥 Fossils and Geologic Time Review Cards

Come Learn with Me: The Fossil Record and the History of Life by Bridget Anderson

---

LEARN
Activity 1: Review the Book *(Offline)*

How much do you remember about fossils and geologic time? Look back through the book to review the things you have learned about the different eras in Earth's early history.

Instructions

Take a moment to look back through the book. Look at the pictures. Can you explain what is shown in each? After you have looked at each picture, review the glossary for words you learned during the unit.

Now use your knowledge of fossils and geologic time to answer each clue on the cards. Write your answer below each question on the solid line at the bottom of the card. After you have answered all the questions, check your answers. Correct any errors you may have made.

Now play a game with the cards. Cut out the cards, then cut each card in half on the dotted line. Turn the cards face down and arrange them in a square of four rows and four columns. Turn one card over and read it to yourself. Then turn another card over. Do they match? You are looking for a question and its answer. If they are not a match, turn them back over and repeat with two new cards. Play close attention to where the you place the cards--it may help you make a match!

The game is over when you have matched all the cards.

ASSESS

Unit Assessment: Fossils and Geologic Time (*Offline*)

Complete an offline Unit Assessment. Your learning coach will score this part of the Assessment.

LEARN

Activity 2. Optional: ZlugQuest Measurement (*Online*)

Fossils and Geologic Time Review Cards

I am a supercontinent. I formed during the Paleozoic era and broke apart in the Mesozoic era. What am I? Answer: _____	I am a fossil. I am made of dead wood that has hardened into stone. What kind of fossil am I? Answer: _____
I am an era in geologic time. In this time, humans created tools and formed communities. Which era am I? Answer: _____	The Earth was just a ball of gases and hot lava when I began. Later, cyanobacteria filled the water. Which period of geological time am I? Answer: _____
When a rock hardens inside a mold fossil, I am formed. What kind of fossil am I? Answer: _____	Velociraptors, proceratopses, and other dinosaurs roamed the Earth during my time period. Which era am I? Answer: _____
I hold an imprint of the shape and texture of something ancient. I may have been mud that has hardened into stone. What kind of fossil am I? Answer: _____	I provide evidence of organisms that are now extinct. By studying me, scientists can reconstruct the history of the Earth. What am I? Answer: _____

Name _____ Date _____

Unit Assessment

Read each question and circle the letter next to the correct answer.

1. Which of these events occurred during the Precambrian time?
   A. Pangaea, the super continent, was formed.
   B. Cyanobacteria filled the water and air with oxygen.
   C. Pangaea began to break apart into many continents separated by shallow seas.
   D. Early humans began to make tools, harvest plants, and make cave paintings.

2. Which of these events occurred during the Paleozoic era?
   A. Pangaea, the super continent, was formed.
   B. Cyanobacteria filled the water and air with oxygen.
   C. Pangaea began to break apart into many continents separated by shallow seas.
   D. Early humans began to make tools, harvest plants, and make cave paintings.

3. Which of these events occurred during the Mesozoic era?
   A. Pangaea, the super continent, was formed.
   B. Cyanobacteria filled the water and air with oxygen.
   C. Pangaea began to break apart into many continents separated by shallow seas.
   D. Early humans began to make tools, harvest plants, and make cave paintings.

4. Which of these events occurred during the Cenozoic era?
   A. Pangaea, the super continent, was formed.
   B. Cyanobacteria filled the water and air with oxygen.
   C. Pangaea began to break apart into many continents separated by shallow seas.
   D. Early humans began to make tools, harvest plants, and make cave paintings.

Name _____ Date _____

Unit Assessment

5. Scientists divide time into four main sections. Two sections are the Precambrian and the Paleozoic. What are the other two sections?
   A. Triassic and Cenzoic
   B. Pennsylvanian and Mesozoic
   C. Ice Age and Precambrian
   D. Cenozoic and Mesozoic

6. Which type of fossil can be described as dead wood that has turned into stone?
   A. cast fossil
   B. mold fossil
   C. sedimentary fossil
   D. petrified

7. Which type of fossil is an imprint made by an organism that was preserved in rock?
   A. cast fossil
   B. mold fossil
   C. sedimentary fossil
   D. petrified

8. Which type of fossil is formed when a rock hardens inside a mold fossil?
   A. cast fossil
   B. mold fossil
   C. sedimentary fossil
   D. petrified

Unit Assessment

9. TRUE or FALSE: Fossils provide evidence that many kinds of organisms that are now extinct once lived on Earth.
   A. True
   B. False

10. TRUE or FALSE: Fossils provide information about organisms that lived long ago and help scientists reconstruct the history of life on Earth.
    A. True
    B. False

Student Guide
Lesson 7: Semester Review and Assessment

Your student will review concepts and skills learned during the semester and then take the second semester assessment.

Lesson Objectives

- Demonstrate mastery of the semester's content.
- Demonstrate mastery of the skills taught in this unit.
- Identify death and emigration as the two main factors that cause a decrease in a population.
- Explain that fossils provide information about organisms that lived long ago.
- State that a *fossil* is a trace, print, or remain of an organism preserved over time in a rock.
- Identify the conditions under which fossils may form.
- Explain that fossils help scientists reconstruct the history of life on Earth.
- State that fossils provide evidence that many kinds of organisms that once lived on Earth are now extinct.
- Identify the different types of fossils, such as petrified, cast, and mold.
- State that geologic time is divided into four sections: Precambrian, Paleozoic, Mesozoic, and Cenozoic.
- Recognize that scientists think that many kinds of organisms once lived on Earth have completely disappeared.
- Recognize that scientists think that some organisms alive today resemble organisms of the distant past.
- Name one major event that occurred during the Precambrian time.
- Name one major event that occurred during the Paleozoic era.
- Name one organism that lived on the Earth during the Precambrian time.
- Name one organism that lived on the Earth during the Paleozoic era.
- Name one major event that occurred during the Mesozoic era.
- Name one major event that occurred during the Cenozoic era.
- Name one organism that lived on the Earth during the Mesozoic era.
- Name one major event that occurred in each of the four geologic sections: Precambrian, Paleozoic, Mesozoic, and Cenozoic.
- Describe the conditions under which fossils may form and distinguish among the different types, such as petrified, mold, and cast.
- Explain that fossils provide information about organisms that lived long ago and help scientists reconstruct the history of life on Earth.
- Recognize that scientists divide geologic time into four main sections (Precambrian, Paleozoic, Mesozoic, and Cenozoic) and that each section covers one major stage in Earth's history.
- Identify characteristics of sponges (they have the ability to regenerate damaged parts, they reproduce through budding, and they live only in water).
- Identify a characteristic of cnidarians (they have tentacles with stinging cells).
- Identify characteristics of roundworms (they bend from side to side to move, have nostrils but no eyes).

- Identify characteristics of mollusks (they have a soft body, a thick skin called a mantle, and a foot for movement).
- Identify common characteristics of arthropods (they have jointed legs, a segmented body, and an exoskeleton).
- Identify characteristics of echinoderms (they are protected by hard plates, their body has radial symmetry, and they move by pumping water into their tube feet).
- Recognize that objects with the same electrical charges repel and objects with different electrical charges attract.
- Explain how to construct a temporary magnet.
- State that electric currents flow easily through materials that are conductors and do not flow easily through materials that are insulators.
- State that electric current produces magnetic fields and that an electromagnet can be made by wrapping a wire around a piece of iron and then running electricity through the wire.
- Identify the four main layers of the Earth and describe their characteristics.
- Recognize that you can identify minerals by their color, luster, hardness, streak, and specific gravity.
- Identify the three different types of rocks and how they form.
- Identify the main parts of a volcano: magma chamber, vent, and crater.
- Identify and describe the three types of land volcanoes (cinder cone, composite, and shield).
- State that an *earthquake* is the shaking or sliding of the Earth's surface.
- Describe a soil profile and explain how different horizons are formed.
- Explain both the physical and the chemical weathering of rocks, and be able to classify examples of each.
- Demonstrate that magnets have two poles (north and south) and that like poles repel each other while unlike poles attract each other.

PREPARE

Approximate lesson time is 60 minutes.

Advance Preparation

- If you don't already have it, you will need the books *Come Learn With Me: Animals Without Backbones - Invertebrates* and *Come Learn With Me: Fossil Record and the History of Life* by Bridget Anderson for the required Explore activity in this lesson.

LEARN
Activity 1: Semester Review *(Online)*

ASSESS

Semester Assessment: Science 4, Semester Two (*Offline*)

Complete an offline Semester Assessment. Your learning coach will score this part of the assessment.

Name _____ Date _____

Semester Assessment

Study the pictures below. In each picture, a type of physical or chemical weathering is taking place. Under each picture, write the name of what is causing the weathering or erosion to occur (water, wind, acids, or glaciers) and whether it is an example of physical or chemical weathering.

1. kind of weathering _____

   What caused the erosion? _____

2. kind of weathering _____

   What caused the erosion? _____

3. kind of weathering _____

   What caused the erosion? _____

4. kind of weathering _____

   What caused the erosion? _____

Semester Assessment

Circle the correct answers for questions 5 – 17.

5. What is name of the towering volcanoes that form from both lava flows and cinder rocks?
   A. cinder cone volcanoes
   B. composite volcanoes
   C. mountain volcanoes
   D. shield volcanoes

6. Scientists divide time into four main sections. Two sections are the Precambrian and the Paleozoic. What are the other two sections?
   A. Triassic and Cenozoic
   B. Pennsylvanian and Mesozoic
   C. Ice Age and Precambrian
   D. Cenozoic and Mesozoic

7. What will happen when the north pole of a magnet is placed against the south pole of another magnet?
   A. The poles will attract each other.
   B. Both magnets will start to spin.
   C. The poles will repel each other.
   D. Both magnets will flip to the opposite side.

8. Which layer of the Earth is extremely hot and made almost entirely of solid iron?
   A. outer core
   B. crust
   C. inner core
   D. mantle

9. What is the tube-like part of a volcano called that lava flows through during an eruption?
   A. magma chamber
   B. cinder cone
   C. crater
   D. vent

Semester Assessment

10. Earthquakes happen around the world and can cause landslides, cracks in the ground, or damage to buildings and roads. Which of the following causes earthquakes?
    A. giant ocean waves called tsunamis
    B. underground movement of earth's plates
    C. energy released from a volcano
    D. problems in the air that make earth unbalanced

11. Scientists can identify common minerals by testing their physical properties. Circle all of the tests that scientists use to do this.
    A. color
    B. smoothness
    C. streak
    D. luster
    E. solubility
    F. hardness

12. True or False: A cast fossil is formed when a rock hardens inside a petrified fossil.

13. True or False: An iron nail can be made magnetic by wrapping it in wire and sending electricity through it.

14. True or False: A needle rubbed with a magnet becomes a permanent magnet.

15. True or False: The crust is the thick, soft, smooth outer layer of the Earth.

16. True or False: The outer core is mostly made of liquid iron.

17. True of False: A cinder cone volcano is formed when lava comes up out of the ground very quickly.

Semester Assessment

Use the words in the Word Bank to complete the sentences below.

chamber	cast	attract
insulators	repel	magnetic
mantle	petrified	profile
inner core	conductors	

18. Objects with the same electrical charges _____, while those with different electric charges _____.

19. Conductors are materials that electric currents flow easily through. Electric currents do not flow easily through _____.

20. Electric currents produce _____fields.

21. If you dig a deep hole in the surface of the Earth, you would see different layers that have formed as a result of many years of weathering. The layers make up the soil _____.

22. A _____fossil is dead wood that has turned into stone.

23. The _____is located between the outer core and the crust. It is made of solid rock, but is under so much pressure that it is constantly moving.

24. The central collecting place for magma at the base of a volcano is called the magma _____.

Semester Assessment

25. Match the groups of invertebrates to their descriptions.

arthropods ○

sponges ○

cnidarians ○

mollusks ○

echinoderms ○

worms ○

○ Protected by hard plates, these animals' bodies show radial symmetry. They pump water into their tube-like feet to move.

○ These animals have nostrils, but no eyes. They bend from side to side to move.

○ The bodies of these animals are segmented and covered in a hard exoskeleton. They have jointed legs.

○ Thick skin covers these animals' soft bodies. They have a foot that is used for movement.

○ These animals have hair and fur to cover their bodies. They also regulate their body temperatures.

○ The ocean is home to these animals. They have tentacles coming from their bodies with long, stinging cells on the ends.

○ These animals are only found in water. They reproduce through budding and have the ability to regenerate a damaged body part.

Semester Assessment

Igneous, sedimentary and metamorphic are the three types of rock found on Earth. Describe each type of rock below and how it is formed.

26. igneous: _____

_____

_____

_____

27. sedimentary: _____

_____

_____

_____

_____

28. metamorphic: _____

_____

_____

_____

_____